RUSSIAN LYRICS

RUSSIAN LYRICS

with Notes and Vocabulary

by

J. D. DUFF, M.A.
Fellow of Trinity College

Cambridge:
at the University Press
1917

CAMBRIDGE
UNIVERSITY PRESS

University Printing House, Cambridge CB2 8BS, United Kingdom

Published in the United States of America by Cambridge University Press, New York

Cambridge University Press is part of the University of Cambridge.

It furthers the University's mission by disseminating knowledge in the pursuit of education, learning and research at the highest international levels of excellence.

www.cambridge.org
Information on this title: www.cambridge.org/9781107646926

First published 1917
First paperback edition 2014

A catalogue record for this publication is available from the British Library

ISBN 978-1-107-64692-6 Paperback

PREFACE

THERE are many good reasons for learning Russian; and those who wish to learn it will do well to read as much poetry as possible. For the best Russian poetry is not inferior to the best Russian prose; and also, while the accent is, after the alphabet, the beginner's chief stumbling-block, in Russian verse the accent of almost every word is indicated by the metre.

I have printed here the text of twenty-five short poems, choosing what I liked best from Púshkin, Lérmontov, Koltsóv, and Alexéi Tolstói, with one poem of Shishkóv, one of Turgénev, and one of Nádson. Each of these little poems is a masterpiece of its kind. The accents have been marked, in the text and elsewhere: until he has made considerable progress, a beginner ought, if possible, never even to see a Russian word unaccented.

The Vocabulary contains all the words in the text; and some words are given under more than one heading. Here the prefixes are in general indicated by hyphens, as experience shows that beginners have much difficulty in discovering the root of each word for themselves; thus, to a boy beginning Greek, *προ-κατα-λαμβάνειν* is less formidable than the undivided word.

The Notes assume some knowledge of elementary grammar. But not much knowledge is taken for granted, and explanation is offered of everything that seemed likely to puzzle a reader fairly familiar with the noun, adjective, and pronoun. Some hints are given on pronunciation; and there is a short biographical note on each of the poets represented in the text. Points of importance have been stated more than once, and there are many references from one passage in the text to another.

There are two short Appendices. The first deals with the Aspects of the verb. If Accent is the first lion in the path, Aspect is the second; yet to read Russian and to ignore Aspects, is to study *Hamlet* with the part of Hamlet left out. Hence the Notes are full of the words 'perfective' and 'imperfective' (for which, but for tradition, I should like to substitute 'aorist' and 'imperfect'). But this seemed insufficient; and therefore, in this Appendix, a perfective verb, of the simplest kind, is compared in detail with its imperfective. A student who has mastered this will still have much to learn about Aspects, but I hope that he will have nothing to unlearn. For refreshment, he can turn to the second Appendix, which contains two translations by the Hon. Maurice Baring; I am grateful to him and his publishers for permission to reprint here these excellent renderings.

I have made much use of Mr Nevill Forbes's *Russian Grammar* (Oxford 1914) and Garbell's *Das russische Zeitwort* (Berlin 1901), and I owe something to Abicht's *Hauptschwierigkeiten der russischen Sprache* (Leipzig 1897); but my chief acknowledgements are due to that admirable work of learning and scholarship known as Boyer and Speranski's *Russian Reader* (Chicago edition).

I should like to add a word of encouragement. Most people speak of Russian as if it were hardly possible for English people to learn it; but I believe this to be a mistake. For nearly two years I have been teaching Russian to University students, and I am sure that a useful knowledge of the language can be acquired in much less time than is generally supposed.

J. D. DUFF.

February, 1917.

CONTENTS

I.

ВЕСЕННІЯ ВОДЫ.

Ещё въ поля́хъ бѣлѣетъ снѣгъ,
А во́ды ужъ весно́й шумя́тъ,
Бѣгу́тъ и бу́дятъ со́нный брегъ,
Бѣгу́тъ и бле́щутъ и глася́тъ.

Онѣ глася́тъ во всѣ концы́: 5
«Весна́ идётъ, весна́ идётъ,
Мы молодо́й весны́ гонцы́,
Она́ насъ вы́слала впередъ!»

Весна́ идётъ, весна́ идётъ,
И ти́хихъ, тёплыхъ, Ма́йскихъ дней 10
Румя́ный свѣ́тлый хорово́дъ
Толпи́тся ве́село за ней!

Tyuchev.

II.

СВЯТАЯ РУСЬ.

Э́ти бѣдныя селе́нья,
Э́та ску́дная приро́да—
Край родно́й долготерпѣнья,
Край ты Ру́сскаго наро́да!

Не поймётъ и не замѣтитъ 5
Го́рдый взоръ иноплеме́нный
Что сквози́тъ и та́йно свѣтитъ
Въ наготѣ твое́й смире́нной.

Удручённый но́шей кре́стной,
Всю тебя́, земля́ родна́я, 10
Въ ра́бскомъ ви́дѣ, Царь Небе́сный
Исходи́лъ благословля́я.

Tyuchev.

III.

ЗАВѢЩАНІЕ.

Наединѣ съ тобо́ю, братъ,
Хотѣлъ бы я побы́ть:
На свѣтѣ ма́ло, говоря́тъ,
Мнѣ остаётся жить!
Поѣдешь ско́ро ты домо́й: 5
Смотри́ жъ...да что! моей судьбо́й,
Сказа́ть по пра́вдѣ, о́чень
Никто́ не озабо́ченъ.

А е́сли спро́ситъ кто́-нибудь...
Ну, кто бы ни спроси́лъ— 10
Скажи́ имъ, что на вы́летъ въ грудь
Я пу́лей ра́ненъ былъ;
Что у́меръ че́стно за царя́,
Что пло́хи на́ши лекаря́,
И что родно́му кра́ю 15
Покло́нъ я посыла́ю.

Отца́ и мать мою́ едва́ ль
Заста́нешь ты въ живы́хъ...
Призна́ться, пра́во, бы́ло бъ жаль
Мнѣ опеча́лить ихъ; 20
Но е́сли кто изъ нихъ и живъ,
Скажи́, что я писа́ть лѣни́въ,
Что полкъ въ похо́дъ посла́ли,
И чтобъ меня́ не жда́ли.

4

Сосѣдка есть у нихъ одна́... 25
Какъ вспо́мнишь, какъ давно́
Разста́лись! О́бо мнѣ она́
Не спро́ситъ. Всё равно́,
Ты разскажи́ всю пра́вду ей,
Пуста́го се́рдца не жалѣ́й— 30
Пуска́й она́ попла́четъ...
Ей ничего́ не зна́читъ!

Lermontov.

IV.

АНЧАРЪ.

Въ пустынѣ ча́хлой и скупо́й,
На по́чвѣ зно́емъ раскалённой,
Анча́ръ, какъ гро́зный часово́й,
Стои́тъ, оди́нъ во всей вселе́нной.

Приро́да жа́ждущихъ степе́й — 5
Его́ въ день гнѣва породи́ла
И зе́лень мёртвую вѣтве́й
И ко́рни я́домъ напои́ла.

Ядъ ка́плетъ сквозь его́ кору́,
Къ полу́дню растопя́сь отъ зно́ю, — 10
И застыва́етъ ввечеру́
Густо́й, прозра́чною смоло́ю.

Къ нему́ и пти́ца не лети́тъ,
И тигръ нейдётъ; лишь ви́хорь чёрный
На дре́во сме́рти набѣжи́тъ— — 15
И мчи́тся прочь уже́ тлетво́рный.

И е́сли ту́ча ороси́тъ,
Блужда́я, листъ его́ дрему́чій,
Съ его́ вѣтве́й ужъ ядови́тъ
Стека́етъ дождь въ песо́къ горю́чій. — 20

Но человѣка человѣкъ
Посла́лъ къ Анча́ру вла́стнымъ взгля́домъ—
И тотъ послу́шно въ путь потёкъ,
И къ у́тру возврати́лся съ я́домъ.

Принёсъ онъ смéртную смолу́, 25
Да вѣтвь съ увя́дшими листáми—
И потъ по блѣдному челу́
Струи́лся хлáдными ручья́ми.

Принёсъ—и ослабѣлъ, и лёгъ
Подъ сво́домъ шалашá, на лы́ки, 30
И у́меръ бѣдный рабъ у ногъ
Непобѣди́маго влады́ки.

А царь тѣмъ я́домъ напитáлъ
Свои́ послу́шливыя стрѣлы,
И съ ни́ми ги́бель разослáлъ 35
Къ сосѣдамъ въ чу́ждые предѣлы.

Pushkin.

V.

КАЗАЧЬЯ КОЛЫБЕЛЬНАЯ ПѢСНЯ.

Спи, младе́нецъ мой прекра́сный,
Ба́юшки-баю́.
Ти́хо смо́тритъ мѣ́сяцъ я́сный
Въ колыбе́ль твою́.
Ста́ну ска́зывать я ска́зки, 5
Пѣ́сенку спою́;
Ты жъ дремли́, закры́вши гла́зки,
Ба́юшки-баю́.

По камня́мъ струи́тся Те́рекъ,
Пле́щетъ му́тный валъ; 10
Злой Чече́нъ ползётъ на бе́регъ,
То́читъ свой кинжа́лъ;
Но оте́цъ твой—ста́рый во́инъ,
Закалёнъ въ бою́;
Спи, малю́тка, будь споко́енъ, 15
Ба́юшки-баю́.

Самъ узна́ешь—бу́детъ вре́мя—
Бра́нное житьё;
Смѣ́ло вдѣ́нешь но́гу въ стре́мя
И возьмёшь ружьё. 20
Я сѣде́льце боево́е
Шо́лкомъ разошью́...
Спи, дитя́ моё родно́е,
Ба́юшки-баю́.

Богаты́рь ты бу́дешь съ ви́ду 25
И каза́къ душо́й.
Провожа́ть тебя́ я вы́йду—
Ты махнёшь руко́й...
Ско́лько го́рькихъ слёзъ укра́дкой
Я въ ту ночь пролью́! 30
Спи, мой а́нгелъ, ти́хо, сла́дко,
Ба́юшки-баю́.

Ста́ну я тоско́й томи́ться,
Безуте́шно ждать;
Ста́ну це́лый день моли́ться, 35
По ноча́мъ гада́ть;
Ста́ну ду́мать, что скуча́ешь
Ты въ чужо́мъ краю́.
Спи жъ, пока́ забо́тъ не зна́ешь,
Ба́юшки-баю́. 40

Дамъ тебе́ я на доро́гу
Образо́къ свято́й;
Ты его́, моля́ся Бо́гу,
Ста́вь пе́редъ собо́й;
Да, гото́вясь въ бо́й опа́сный, 45
По́мни мать свою́.
Спи, младе́нецъ мой прекра́сный,
Ба́юшки-баю́.

Lermontov.

VI.

АРЗРУМЪ.

Стамбу́лъ гяу́ры ны́нче сла́вятъ,
А за́втра ко́ваной пято́й,
Какъ змія спя́щаго разда́вятъ,
И прочь пойду́тъ—и такъ оста́вятъ:
Стамбу́лъ засну́лъ пе́редъ бѣдо́й. 5

Стамбу́лъ отрёкся отъ Проро́ка;
Въ нёмъ пра́вду дре́вняго Восто́ка
Лука́вый За́падъ омрачи́лъ;
Стамбу́лъ, для сла́достей поро́ка,
Мольбѣ и са́блѣ измѣни́лъ; 10
Стамбу́лъ отвы́къ отъ по́ту би́твы,
И пьётъ вино́ въ часы́ моли́твы.

Въ нёмъ вѣ́ры чи́стой лучъ поту́хъ;
Въ нёмъ жёны по база́ру хо́дятъ,
На перекрёстки шлютъ стару́хъ, 15
А тѣ мужчи́нъ въ гаре́мы вво́дятъ,
И спитъ подку́пленный евну́хъ.

Но не тако́въ Арзру́мъ наго́рный,
Многодоро́жный нашъ Арзру́мъ:
Не спимъ мы въ ро́скоши позо́рной, 20
Ни че́рплемъ ча́шей непоко́рной
Въ винѣ́ развра́тъ, ого́нь и шумъ.

Пости́мся мы; струёю тре́звой
Одни́ фонта́ны насъ поя́тъ;
Толпо́й неистовой и рѣ́звой 25
Джиги́ты на́ши въ бой летя́тъ;
Мы къ жёнамъ какъ орлы́ ревни́вы,
Гаре́мы на́ши молчали́вы,
Непроница́емы стоя́тъ.

Pushkin.

VII.

ТАЛИСМАНЪ.

Тамъ гдѣ мо́ре вѣ́чно пле́щетъ
На пусты́нныя скалы́,
Гдѣ луна́ теплѣе бле́щетъ
Въ сла́дкій часъ вече́рней мглы,
Гдѣ въ гаре́махъ наслажда́ясь, 5
Дни прово́дитъ мусульма́нъ;
Тамъ волше́бница, ласка́ясь,
Мнѣ вручи́ла талисма́нъ.

И ласка́ясь говори́ла:
«Сохрани́ мой талисма́нъ— 10
Въ нёмъ таинственная си́ла!
Онъ тебѣ любо́вью данъ.
Отъ неду́га, отъ моги́лы,
Въ бу́рю, въ гро́зный урага́нъ,
Головы́ твое́й, мой ми́лый, 15
Не спасётъ мой талисма́нъ.

И бога́тствами Восто́ка
Онъ тебя́ не одари́тъ,
И покло́нниковъ Проро́ка
Онъ тебѣ не покори́тъ; 20
И тебя́ на ло́но дру́га,
Отъ печа́льныхъ чу́ждыхъ стра́нъ
Въ край родно́й, на сѣ́веръ съ ю́га,
Не умчи́тъ мой талисма́нъ.

Но когда́ кова́рны о́чи 25
Очару́ютъ вдругъ тебя́,
Иль уста́ во мра́кѣ но́чи
Поцѣлу́ютъ, не любя́:
Ми́лый другъ! отъ преступле́нья,
Отъ серде́чныхъ но́выхъ ранъ, 30
Отъ измѣны, отъ забве́нья
Сохрани́тъ мой талисма́нъ.»

Pushkin.

VIII.

СЕРЕНАДА.

У стѣны́ твое́й высо́кой,
Подъ завѣшеннымъ окно́мъ,
Я стою́ въ тѣни́ широ́кой,
Весь оку́танный плащёмъ.

Звѣзды блещутъ, стра́стью ди́вной 5
Ды́шетъ го́лосъ соловья́;
Вы́йдь, о, вы́йдь на звукъ призы́вной,
Появи́сь, звѣзда́ моя́!

Ско́лько бъ мы пото́мъ ни жи́ли,
Я хочу́, чтобъ мы съ тобо́й 10
До моги́лы не забы́ли
Э́той но́чи огнево́й.

И легко́ и тороплво,
Сло́вно при́зракъ, чуть дыша́,
Озира́ясь боязли́во, 15
Ты сойдёшь ко мнѣ, душа́!

Безконе́чно торжеству́я,
Устремлю́сь я на крыльцо́,
На колѣни упаду́ я,
Посмотрю́ тебѣ въ лицо́. 20

И зати́хнетъ ро́бкій тре́петъ,
И пройдётъ послѣдній страхъ,
И замрётъ твой дѣтскій ле́петъ
На преда́вшихся губа́хъ.

Иль ты спишь, сложи́вши ру́ки, 25
И не по́мнишь о́бо мнѣ,
И напра́сно льются звуки
Въ благово́нной тишинѣ?

Turgenev.

IX.

ПѢСНЯ.

Я люби́ла его́
Жа́рче дня и огня́,
Какъ други́мъ не люби́ть
Никогда́, никогда́!

То́лько съ нимъ лишь одни́мъ — 5
Я на свѣтѣ жила́;
Ему́ ду́шу мою́,
Ему́ жизнь отдала́!

Что за ночь, за луна́,
Когда́ дру́га я жду! — 10
Вся блѣдна́, холодна́,
Замира́ю, дрожу́.

Вотъ идётъ онъ, поётъ:
«Гдѣ ты, зо́рька моя́?»
Вотъ онъ ру́ку берётъ, — 15
Вотъ цѣлу́етъ меня́!

«Ми́лый другъ, погаси́
Поцѣлу́и твой!
И безъ нихъ, при тебѣ,
Огнь пыла́етъ въ крови́; — 20

И безъ нихъ, при тебѣ,
Жжётъ румя́нецъ лицо́,
И волну́ется грудь,
И блиста́ютъ глаза́,
Сло́вно въ не́бѣ звѣзда́!» — 25

Koltsov.

X.

ДУХЪ БЕРЕЗЫ.

То бы́ло ра́ннею весно́й,
Трава́ едва́ всходи́ла,
Ручьи́ текли́, не па́рилъ зной,
И зе́лень рощъ сквози́ла;

Труба́ пасту́шья поутру́ 5
Ещё не пѣла зво́нко,
И въ завитка́хъ ещё въ бору́
Былъ па́поротникъ то́нкій;

То бы́ло ра́ннею весно́й,
Въ тѣни́ берёзъ то бы́ло, 10
Когда́ съ улы́бкой пре́до мной
Ты о́чи опусти́ла...

То на любо́вь мою́ въ отвѣтъ
Ты опусти́ла вѣжды—
О жизнь! о лѣсъ! о со́лнца свѣтъ! 15
О ю́ность! о наде́жды!

И пла́калъ я пе́редъ тобо́й,
На ликъ твой глядя ми́лый—
То бы́ло ра́ннею весно́й,
Въ тѣни́ берёзъ то бы́ло! 20

То было въ у́тро на́шихъ лѣтъ—
О сча́стіе! о слёзы!
О лѣсъ! о жизнь! о со́лнца свѣтъ!
О свѣ́жій духъ берёзы!

A. Tolstoi.

XI.

СМЕРТЬ.

Когда́ я ста́ну умира́ть—
И вѣрь, тебѣ не до́лго ждать—
Ты перене́сть меня́ вели́
Въ нашъ садъ, въ то мѣсто, гдѣ цвѣли́
Ака́цій бѣлыхъ два куста́... 5
Трава́ межъ ни́ми такъ густа́,
И свѣжій во́здухъ такъ души́стъ,
И такъ прозра́чно золоти́стъ
Игра́ющій на со́лнцѣ листъ!
Тамъ положи́ть вели́ меня́. 10
Сія́ньемъ голуба́го дня
Упью́ся я въ послѣдній разъ.
Отту́да ви́денъ и Кавка́зъ!
Быть мо́жетъ, онъ съ свои́хъ высо́тъ
Привѣтъ проща́льный мнѣ пришлётъ, 15
Пришлётъ съ прохла́днымъ вѣтерко́мъ...
И близъ меня́ пе́редъ концо́мъ
Родно́й опя́ть разда́стся звукъ!
И ста́ну ду́мать я, что другъ
Иль братъ, склони́вшись на́до мной, 20
Отёръ съ внима́тельной руко́й
Съ лица́ кончи́ны хла́дный потъ,
И что въ полго́лоса поётъ
Онъ мнѣ про ми́лую страну́;
И съ э́той мы́слью я засну́, 25
И никого́ не прокляну́!

Lermontov.

XII.

НА СМЕРТНОМЪ ОДРѢ.

Весь день она́ лежа́ла въ забытьи́,
И всю её ужъ тѣни покрыва́ли;
Лилъ тёплый лѣтній дождь, его́ струи́
По ли́стьямъ ве́село звуча́ли.

И ме́дленно опо́мнилась она́, 5
И начала́ прислу́шиваться къ шу́му,
И до́лго слу́шала—увлечена́,
Погружена́ въ созна́тельную ду́му.

И вотъ, какъ бы бесѣдуя съ собо́й,
Созна́тельно она́ проговори́ла 10
(Я былъ при ней, уби́тый но живо́й):
«О, какъ всё э́то я люби́ла!»

Люби́ла ты, и такъ какъ ты люби́ть—
Нѣтъ, никому́ ещё не удава́лось!
О Го́споди!... и э́то пережи́ть!... 15
И се́рдце на клочки́ не разорва́лось!

Tyuchev.

XIII.

КОЛОДНИКИ.

Спуска́ется со́лнце за сте́пи,
Вдали́ золоти́тся ковы́ль,—
Коло́дниковъ зво́нкія цѣпи
Взмета́ютъ доро́жную пыль.

Иду́тъ они́ съ бри́тыми лба́ми, 5
Шага́ютъ вперёдъ тяжело́,
Угрю́мыя сдви́нули бро́ви,
На се́рдце разду́мье легло́.

Иду́тъ съ ни́ми дли́нныя тѣни,
Двѣ кля́чи телѣгу везу́тъ, 10
Лѣни́во сгиба́я колѣни,
Конво́йные съ ни́ми иду́тъ.

—Что, бра́тцы, затя́немте пѣсню,
Забу́демъ лиху́ю бѣду́!
Ужъ ви́дно така́я невзго́да 15
Напи́сана намъ на роду́!

И вотъ, повели́, затяну́ли,
Пою́тъ, залива́ясь, они́
Про Во́лги широ́кой раздо́лье,
Про да́ромъ мину́вшіе дни; 20

Пою́тъ про свобо́дныя сте́пи,
Про ди́кую во́лю пою́тъ,
День ме́ркнетъ всё бо́лѣ,—а цѣпи
Доро́гу мету́тъ да мету́тъ.

A. Tolstoi.

XIV.

ДОРОЖНАЯ КАРТИНА.

По гре́блѣ неро́вной и тря́ской,
Вдоль мо́крыхъ рыба́чьихъ сѣте́й,
Доро́жная ѣдетъ коля́ска,
Сижу́ я заду́мчиво въ ней;

Сижу́ и смотрю́ я доро́гой 5
На сѣрый и па́смурный день,
На о́зера бе́регъ отло́гій,
На да́льній дымо́къ дереве́нь.

По гре́блѣ, со взгля́домъ угрю́мымъ
Прохо́дитъ изо́рванный жидъ; 10
Изъ о́зера съ пѣной и шу́момъ
Вода́ че́резъ гре́блю бѣжи́тъ;

Тамъ ма́льчикъ игра́етъ на ду́дкѣ,
Забра́вшись въ зелёный тростни́къ;
Въ испу́гѣ взлетѣвшія у́тки 15
Надъ о́зеромъ по́дняли крикъ;

Близъ ме́льницы ста́рой и ша́ткой
Сидя́тъ на травѣ мужики́;
Телѣга съ разби́той лоша́дкой
Лѣни́во подво́зитъ мѣшки́. 20

Мнѣ ка́жется всё такъ знако́мо,
Хоть не́ былъ я здѣсь никогда́,
И кры́ша далёкаго до́ма,
И ма́льчикъ, и лѣсъ, и вода́,

И ме́льницы го́воръ уны́лый 25
И ве́тхое въ по́лѣ гумно́,
Всё э́то когда́-то ужъ бы́ло
Но мно́ю забы́то давно́.

Такъ то́чно ступа́ла лоша́дка,
Такі́е-жъ тащи́ла мѣшки́; 30
Такі́е-жъ у ме́льницы ша́ткой
Сидѣли въ травѣ мужики́;

И такъ же шёлъ жидъ борода́тый,
И такъ же шумѣла вода́—
Все э́то ужъ бы́ло когда́-то, 35
Но то́лько не по́мню когда́.

A. Tolstoi.

XV.

ВЕСНА.

Зимá не дáромъ злúтся:
Прошлá ея́ порá;
Веснá въ окнó стучúтся
И гóнитъ со дворá.

И всё засуетúлось, 5
Всё гóнитъ зúму вонъ,
И жáворонки въ нéбѣ
Ужъ пóдняли трезвóнъ.

Зимá ещё хлопóчетъ
И на веснý ворчúтъ, 10
Та ей въ глазá хохóчетъ
И пýще лишь шумúтъ!

Взбѣсúлась вѣдьма злáя
И, снѣгу захватя́,
Пустúла, убѣгáя, 15
Въ прекрáсное дитя́.

Веснѣ и гóря мáло:
Умы́лася въ снѣгý,
И лишь румя́нѣй стáла
Наперекóръ врагý. 20

Tyuchev.

XVI.

ПЕРВЫЙ ЛИСТЪ.

Листъ зеленѣетъ молодо́й.
Смотри́, какъ ли́стьемъ молоды́мъ
Стоя́тъ обвѣяны берёзы,
Возду́шной зе́ленью сквозно́й,
Полу-прозра́чною какъ дымъ. 5

Давно́ имъ гре́зилось весно́й,
Весно́й и лѣтомъ золоты́мъ,
И вотъ живы́я э́ти грёзы,
Подъ пе́рвымъ не́бомъ голубы́мъ,
Проби́лись вдругъ на свѣтъ дневно́й. 10

О, пе́рвыхъ ли́стьевъ красота́,
Омы́тыхъ въ со́лнечныхъ луча́хъ,
Съ новорождённою ихъ тѣнью!
И слы́шно намъ по ихъ движе́нью
Что въ э́тихъ ты́сячахъ и тьмахъ 15
Не встрѣтишь мёртваго листа́.

Tyuchev.

XVII.

ТУЧА.

Послѣдняя ту́ча разсѣянной бу́ри!
Одна́ ты несёшься по я́сной лазу́ри,
Одна́ ты наво́дишь уны́лую тѣнь,
Одна́ ты печа́лишь лику́ющій день.

Ты не́бо неда́вно круго́мъ облега́ла, 5
И мо́лнія гро́зно тебя́ обвива́ла,
И ты издава́ла таинственный громъ,
И а́лчную зе́млю поила дождёмъ.

Дово́льно, сокро́йся! Пора́ минова́лась,
Земля́ освѣжи́лась и бу́ря промча́лась, 10
И вѣтеръ, ласка́я листо́чки древе́съ,
Тебя́ съ успоко́енныхъ го́нитъ небе́съ.

Pushkin.

XVIII.

ДУМА СОКОЛА.

До́лго ль бу́ду я
Си́днемъ до́ма жить,
Мою́ мо́лодость
Ни на что́ губи́ть?

До́лго ль бу́ду я 5
Подъ окно́мъ сидѣть,
По доро́гѣ вдаль
День и ночь глядѣть?

Иль у со́кола
Кры́лья свя́заны, 10
Иль пути́ ему́
Всѣ зака́заны?

Иль бои́тся онъ
Въ чужи́хъ людяхъ быть,
Съ судьбо́й-ма́чихой 15
Самъ-собо́ю жить?

Для чего́ на́ свѣтъ
Глядѣть хо́чется,
Облетѣть его́
Душа́ про́сится? 20

Иль зачѣмъ она́,
Моя́ ми́лая,
Здѣсь сиди́тъ со мной,
Слёзы льётъ рѣко́й;

Отъ меня́ лети́тъ, 25
Пѣсню мнѣ поётъ,
Всё руко́й мани́тъ,
Всё съ собо́й зовётъ?

Нѣтъ, ужъ по́лно мнѣ
До́ма вѣкъ сидѣть, 30
По доро́жкѣ вдаль
Изъ окна́ глядѣть!

Со двора́ пойду́,
Куда́ пу́ть мани́тъ,
А жить ста́ну тамъ, 35
Гдѣ ужъ Бо́гъ вели́тъ.

Koltsov.

XIX.

БѢДНЫЕ ЛЮДИ.

Не въ нѣгѣ я родился,
Не въ роскоши я жилъ;
Работалъ и трудился
И хладъ и зной сносилъ;
Терпя различны муки, 5
Боролся я съ судьбой;
Мои суровы руки
Не знали, что покой.

Я солнечнаго всходу
Ни разу не проспалъ, 10
Въ суровую погоду
Укрыться не искалъ;
Но плугомъ раздирая
Утробу я земли,
То дрогнулъ промокая, 15
То весь горѣлъ въ пыли.

За разными трудами
Меня зрѣлъ солнца бѣгъ:
Здѣсь твёрдыми стѣнами
Одѣлъ я дикой брегъ; 20
Тамъ каменные домы
Воздвигнулъ для другихъ,
Чуть крышу изъ соломы
Имѣя для своихъ.

Одна́кожъ въ э́то вре́мя, 25
Бывъ мо́лодъ и здоро́въ,
Не чу́вствовалъ я бре́мя
Сихъ тя́гостныхъ трудо́въ;
Безъ вся́каго изли́шку
Дово́льно собира́лъ, 30
Корми́лъ свою́ семьи́шку,
Былъ сытъ и сла́дко спалъ.

Но мла́дость промелькну́ла,
Ея́ ужъ бо́лѣ нѣтъ;
Скорбь лютая согну́ла 35
Упру́гій мой хребе́тъ;
Мой одръ, гдѣ я, страда́я,
Убо́гъ лежу́ и сиръ,
Злой сме́рти ожида́я,
Сталъ ны́нѣ весь мой міръ. 40

A. Shishkov.

XX.

ПТИЧІЙ ГОЛОСЪ.

Дождя́ отшумѣ́вшаго ка́пли
Тихо́нько по ли́стьямъ текли́,
Тихо́нько шепта́лись дере́вья,
Куку́шка крича́ла вдали́.

Луна́ на меня́ изъ-за ту́чи 5
Смотрѣ́ла, какъ бу́дто въ слеза́хъ,
Сидѣ́лъ я подъ клёномъ и ду́малъ,
И ду́малъ о пре́жнихъ года́хъ.

Не зна́ю, была́ ли въ тѣ го́ды
Душа́ непоро́чна моя́, 10
Но мно́гому-бъ я не повѣ́рилъ,
Не сдѣ́лалъ бы мно́гаго я;

Тепе́рь же мнѣ ста́ли поня́тны
Обма́нъ, и кова́рство, и зло,
И мно́гія свѣ́тлыя мысли 15
Одну́ за друго́й унесло́.

Такъ ду́малъ о дняхъ я мину́вшихъ,
О дняхъ, когда́ былъ я добрѣ́й,
А въ ли́стьяхъ высо́каго клёна
Сидѣ́лъ на́до мной солове́й, 20

И пѣлъ онъ такъ нѣ́жно и стра́стно,
Какъ бу́дто хотѣ́лъ онъ сказа́ть:
«Утѣ́шься, не сѣ́туй напра́сно,
То вре́мя вернётся опя́ть.»

A. Tolstoi.

XXI.

ЗИМНІЙ ВЕЧЕРЪ.

Бýря мглóю нéбо крóетъ,
Вúхри снѣжные крутя́:
Тó какъ звѣрь онá завóетъ,
Тó заплáчетъ какъ дитя́,
Тó по крóвлѣ обветшáлой 5
Вдругъ солóмой зашумúтъ,
Тó какъ пýтникъ запоздáлый
Къ намъ въ окóшко застучúтъ.

Нáша вéтхая лачýжка
И печáльна и темнá; 10
Что же ты, моя́ старýшка,
Пріумóлкла у окнá?
Йли бýри завывáньемъ
Ты, мой другъ, утомленá,
Или дрéмлешь подъ жужжáньемъ 15
Своегó веретенá?

Вы́пьемъ, дóбрая подрýжка
Бѣдной юности моéй!
Вы́пьемъ съ гóря; гдѣ же крýжка?
Сéрдцу бýдетъ веселѣ́й. 20
Спой мнѣ пѣсню, какъ синúца
Тúхо зá моремъ жилá;
Спой мнѣ пѣсню, какъ дѣвúца
За водóй поýтру шла.

Бу́ря мгло́ю не́бо кро́етъ, 25
Ви́хри снѣ́жные крутя́:
То́ какъ звѣ́рь она́ зав́оетъ,
То́ запла́четъ какъ дитя́.
Вы́пьемъ, до́брая подру́жка
Бѣ́дной ю́ности мое́й! 30
Вы́пьемъ съ го́ря; гдѣ́ же кру́жка?
Се́рдцу бу́детъ веселѣ́й.

Pushkin.

XXII.

СТАНЦІЯ.

Что́ за гру́стная оби́тель,
И како́й знако́мый видъ!
За стѣно́й храпи́тъ смотри́тель,
Со́нно ма́ятникъ стучи́тъ!

Сту́кнетъ впра́во, сту́кнетъ влѣво, 5
Бу́дитъ мыслей дли́нный рядъ;
Въ нёмъ разска́зы и напѣвы
Затвержённые звуча́тъ.

А въ подсвѣчникѣ пыла́етъ
Догорѣвшая свѣча́, 10
Гдѣ-то пёсъ далёко ла́етъ,
Хо́дитъ ма́ятникъ, стуча́;

Сту́кнетъ влѣво, сту́кнетъ впра́во,
Всё тверди́тъ о старинѣ;
Гру́стно такъ! Не зна́ю, пра́во, 15
На яву́ я иль во снѣ?

Вотъ ужъ ло́шади гото́вы—
Сѣлъ въ киби́тку и скачу́—
По́лно, такъ ли? Ви́жу сно́ва
Ту же са́льную свѣчу́, 20

Ту же гру́стную оби́тель
И круго́мъ знако́мый видъ,
За стѣно́й храпи́тъ смотри́тель,
Со́нно ма́ятникъ стучи́тъ.

A. Tolstoi.

XXIII.

ПОЛНОЧНАЯ ДУМА.

Шуми́тъ на дворѣ́ непого́да,
А въ до́мѣ давно́ уже́ спятъ;
Къ око́шку, вздохну́въ, подхожу́ я:
Чуть ви́денъ чернѣ́ющій садъ;

На не́бѣ такъ тёмно, такъ тёмно, 5
И звѣ́здочки нѣтъ ни одно́й,
А въ до́мѣ стари́нномъ такъ гру́стно
Среди́ непого́ды ночно́й!

Дождь бьётъ, бараба́ня, по кры́шѣ,
Хруста́льныя лю́стры дрожа́тъ, 10
За шка́помъ прово́рныя мы́ши
Въ бума́жныхъ обо́яхъ шумя́тъ;

Онѣ́ себѣ́ чу́ютъ раздо́лье:
Какъ ско́ро хозя́инъ умрётъ,
Наслѣ́дникъ поки́нетъ помѣ́стье, 15
Гдѣ жилъ его́ до́блестный родъ,

И домъ навсегда́ запустѣ́етъ,
Загло́хнутъ ступе́ни траво́й...
И ду́мать объ э́томъ такъ гру́стно
Среди́ непого́ды ночно́й! 20

A. Tolstoi.

XXIV.

ИЗГНАННИКЪ.

Пошли́ Госпо́дь свою́ отра́ду
Тому́, кто въ лѣтній жаръ и зной,
Какъ бѣдный ни́щій, ми́мо са́ду
Бредётъ по жа́ркой мостово́й;

Кто смо́тритъ вскользь че́резъ огра́ду 5
На тѣнь дере́вьевъ, злакъ доли́нъ,
На недосту́пную прохла́ду
Роско́шныхъ свѣтлыхъ догови́нъ.

Не для него́ гостепрі́имной
Дере́вья сѣнью разросли́сь, 10
Не для него́, какъ о́блакъ ды́мной,
Фонта́нъ на во́здухѣ пови́съ.

Лазу́рный гротъ, какъ изъ тума́на,
Напра́сно взоръ его́ мани́тъ,
И пыль роси́стая фонта́на 15
Главы́ его́ не освѣжи́тъ.

Пошли́ Госпо́дь свою́ отра́ду
Тому́, кто жи́зненной тропо́й,
Какъ бѣдный ни́щій ми́мо са́ду,
Бредётъ по зно́йной мостово́й. 20

Tyuchev.

XXV.

ТОРЖЕСТВО ЛЮБВИ.

Другъ мой, братъ мой, усталый, страдающій
братъ,
Кто бъ ты ни былъ, не падай душой:
Пусть неправда и зло полновластно царятъ
Надъ омытой слезами землёй,
Пусть разбитъ и поруганъ святой идеалъ 5
И струится невинная кровь:—
Вѣрь, настанетъ пора, и погибнетъ Ваалъ,
И вернётся на землю любовь!

Не въ терновомъ вѣнцѣ, не подъ гнётомъ
цѣпей,
Не съ крестомъ на согбенныхъ плечахъ,— 10
Въ міръ придётъ она въ силѣ и славѣ своей,
Съ яркимъ свѣточемъ славы въ рукахъ.
И не будетъ на свѣтѣ ни слёзъ, ни вражды,
Ни безкрестныхъ могилъ, ни рабовъ,
Ни нужды безпросвѣтной, мертвящей нужды,
Ни меча, ни позорныхъ столбовъ. 16

О, мой другъ! Не мечтá э́тотъ свѣ́тлый
приxóдъ,
Не пустáя надéжда однá:
Оглянись,—зло вокрýгъ черезчýръ ужъ
гнетётъ,
Ночь вокрýгъ черезчýръ ужъ темнá! 20
Міръ устáнетъ отъ мукъ, захлебнётся въ
кровú,
Утомúтся безýмной борьбóй,—
И поднúметъ къ любвú, къ беззавѣ́тной
любвú,
О́чи, пóлныя скóрбной мольбóй.

Nadson.

NOTES

Most of the abbreviations used will be readily understood: *instr.* stands for the instrumental case, and *loc.* for the locative or prepositional. 'Forbes' refers to Mr Nevill Forbes' *Russian Grammar* (Oxford 1914); 'Boyer' to the *Russian Reader* of Messrs Boyer and Speranski (Chicago *n.d.*).

Verbs are called perfective or imperfective, in the sense that they belong to the perfective or imperfective aspect.

I.

SPRING WATERS.

Theodor Tyúchev (1803–1873) wrote about a hundred short lyric poems and nothing else; but he is a great poet, and I believe that most English readers would prefer his lyrics to Púshkin's. He never writes better than about spring, and three of his spring poems are included here (I, XV, XVI); all are exquisite. For the opinion of a great critic on Tyúchev's poetry, see the prefatory note to XXIV.

Here he describes the rushing of water that inaugurates spring in Russia, when the snow melts and the ice on the rivers breaks up

1 ещё: pronounce *yesh-chó*. (1) At the beginning of a word, е is always preceded by a *y* sound; elsewhere, it may or may not have this sound. (2) When е is accented, it often takes the sound of *o* or *yo*: thus ёжъ, 'hedgehog,' is pronounced *yosh*: in all such cases, it is printed ё in this text.

въ is not a syllable and coalesces entirely with the following word.

2 во́ды, nom. plur., but воды́ gen. sing.: this change of accent is common where the noun is of two syllables and ends in -á; e.g. рука́, hand: gen. sing. руки́; nom. plur. ру́ки.

веснóй, 'with spring,' the original use of the instrumental case: the same case often has a temporal sense, e.g. веснóй, 'in spring'; лѣ́томъ, 'in summer'; óсенью, 'in autumn'; зимóй, 'in winter.'

3 бѣгýтъ, from бѣжáть, an irregular verb, which makes бѣгý, бѣжи́шь, бѣгýтъ, and imperative бѣги́.

бýдятъ, from буди́ть: this change of accent, being very common, should be noted: бужý, 'I awaken,' but бýдишь, 'thou awakenest': it is essential to distinguish between буди́ть (inf.) and бýдитъ (3rd pers. sing.).

брегъ, a contraction of бéрегъ: it occurs again XIX 20.

5 во: въ assumes this form before certain groups of consonants, of which вс- is one.

всѣ концы́, 'all the ends of the earth.'

6 идётъ: pronounce *eed-yót*. Spring is supposed to come on foot; if she came in a chariot, ѣ́детъ (from ѣхать) would be required instead.

7 This clause has no verb, because the equivalents of *am*, *art*, and *are* are omitted in Russian: есть = 'is' is sometimes expressed, e.g. III 25.

мы is subject, гонцы́ predicate.

8 вы́-слала: past perfective, with the sense of our perfect: the same tense does duty for our pluperf. and aorist as well.

11 хоро-вóдъ is properly a gathering of village girls to dance and sing.

12 толпи́т-ся: the last syll., pronounced *-sa* and not *-sya*, is a contraction of себя́ and is a regular suffix of reflexive verbs.

The eye must be trained to distinguish at once толпи́тся (3rd sing. pres. ind.) from толпи́ться (inf.).

за ней, 'after her': ей becomes ней, because, after a preposition, н is prefixed to the oblique cases of онъ, она́, онó: so у негó, за нимъ etc.

II.

HOLY RUSSIA.

The poet says that the foreign eye is not impressed by the Russian landscape and cannot detect the real greatness of Russia which lies in her power to endure suffering like her Divine Master.

2 The dash at the end of the line shows that 'is' must be supplied; it is often used so both in prose and verse: see v 13.

3 край is nom. here but voc. below.

роднóй, nom. sing. masc.: the gen. fem., impossible here, is also роднóй.

The beginner should impress firmly upon his mind, that Russian adjectives are declined throughout the singular, not like nouns (as in Latin), but like pronouns, e.g. онъ or тотъ.

3 and 4 were prefixed by Turgénev as a motto to his Живы́я Мóщи (*Living Relics*).

5 'Will not understand and will not notice': both verbs are present in form, but, as they are perfectives, future in meaning; понимáетъ and замѣчáетъ are the corresponding imperfectives, and they are present in meaning as well as in form. See Appendix I § 4.

6 ино-племéнный, 'foreign,' from инóй, 'other,' and плéмя, 'race': ино-стрáнецъ is the common word for 'foreigner.'

7 что̀: pronounce *shto*: thus accented, it is a relative pron. Distinguish свѣтитъ (3rd pers. pres. ind.) from свѣти́ть (inf.): they differ both in accent and termination.

10 тебя́: acc. governed by исходи́лъ.

12 ис-ходи́лъ, 'travelled through on foot': the prefix gives the sense of 'entirely'; and ходи́ть, like идти́, always implies motion on foot.

благо-словля́я: pres. gerund of благо-словля́ть.

III.

LAST WISHES.

Michael Lérmontov (1814–1841), a Russian of remote Scottish ancestry, was killed in a duel at the age of twenty-six, leaving a considerable amount of lyric verse and a novel (Герóй нáшего врéмени, *A Hero of Our Time*). He was strongly influenced by Byron. His work is unequal; but the best of it is unsurpassed in simplicity, force, and melody.

In this poem, a wounded soldier, dying abroad, expresses his last wishes to a brother-officer. A translation by Mr Maurice Baring will be found in Appendix II.

1 съ тобóю: pronounce as one word—*sta-bó-yu*. Brother-officers, unless they are about to meet in a duel, use the 2nd pers. sing. to one another.

братъ, 'brother,' must be distinguished from брать, 'to take.'

2 хотѣ́лъ бы, 'I should like': бы (or бъ in the contracted form) is the conditional particle, used with the past tense.

по-бы́ть, 'to be for a while': по-, prefixed to a verb, often attenuates its meaning.

3 на свѣ́тѣ belongs to жить: cf. IX 6.

говоря́тъ, 'they say,' 'I am told': this pl. with an indefinite subject is very common and often takes the place of our passive: e.g. царя́ убили, 'the Tsar has been murdered.'

4 остаёт-ся: 3rd pers. sing., pres. ind. of остава́ть-ся: similarly дава́ть (to give) makes даю́, даёшь, даётъ.

5 поѣдешь, 'thou wilt travel' (not on foot, which would be пойдёшь).

Again, the verb, though present in form, is future in meaning, because it is perfective: ѣдешь = 'thou art travelling,' поѣ́дешь = 'thou wilt travel.' Similar perfectives are спро́ситъ (ll. 9 and 28), and за-ста́нешь (l. 18): all three have a future sense. See Appendix I § 4.

6 смотри́ жъ, 'well, look here!': жъ or же is an enclitic particle with many meanings: its commonest use is to emphasise the word before it, e.g. сего́ же дня, 'this very day,' more emphatic than сего́дня.

да что = 'but, after all.'

судьбо́й: pronounce *soo-dybóy* (the first *y* being a consonant): the case (instr.) is due to о-забо́ченъ.

8 никто́ не: even where the subject is negative, the verb must always be negatived also: никто́ изъ нихъ не поги́бъ, 'not one of them was lost.'

9 спро́ситъ: Russian idiom, like Latin, requires the future here: we say, 'If anyone asks....'

Distinguish спро́ситъ from спроси́ть (inf.).

10 кто бы ни, 'whoever' may ask: see VIII 9, XXV 2.

11 имъ: dat. plur.

12 ра́ненъ, 'wounded,' past participle passive of ра́нить.

Every past participle and adjective has two forms: (1) a longer form, when it is used attributively, as до́брый человѣ́къ, 'a good man'; (2) a shorter form, when the adj. or participle is the predicate, as человѣ́къ добръ, 'the man is good.' ра́ненъ, being the predicate here, takes the place of ра́неный. Similar short forms are плóхи (for плохíе) in l. 14, живъ (for живóй) in l. 21, and лѣни́въ (for лѣни́вый) in l. 22.

13 за царя́, 'for the Tsar': a famous opera called Жизнь за Царя́ (*Life for the Tsar*), by Glinka, the first great Russian composer, was produced in 1837.

17 едвá (pronounce *yed-vá*) is often followed by ли (or ль): it means 'I hardly think you will find....'

18 за-стáнешь: pres. ind. of the perfective за-стáть.

19 при-знáться = при-знаю́сь: the inf. is used with much more freedom than in English: see IX 3.

бъ is the contracted form of бы.

As жаль is a fem. noun, the verb should properly be былá, but it is used in such a way as to pass for an adverb: the usual constr. is мнѣ жаль её, 'I am sorry for her.'

21 изъ нихъ: see n. to за ней, I 12.

23 полкъ по-слáли, 'they have sent the regiment,' i.e. 'the regiment has been sent': see n. to l. 3.

Note that что introduces an indirect statement, and чтобъ (i.e. чтó-бы) an indirect command, 'that they must not expect me.'

25 есть: commonly omitted: it does not occur again in these poems.

однá here is merely the indefinite article.

26 'When one thinks, how long ago we (two) parted!' The first какъ has, as often, the sense of когдá.

вспóмнишь, lit. 'thou shalt remember': the 2nd pers. sing. is regularly used where we use 'one,' to generalise a statement: comp. XVI 16.

27 раз-стáлись: supply мы as subject.

30 пустáго: pronounce *pu-stáw-va*, throwing the whole stress on the middle syllable. The gen. is due to the regular rule that the direct object of a negatived verb is in the gen.: ви́дѣли-ли вы её? я не видáлъ ея́, 'Did you see her? I did not see her.'

жалѣ́й: in prohibitions, the imperfective verb is used: hence жалѣ́й and not по-жалѣ́й here, though the perfective раз-скажи́ was used in l. 29: comp. XXV 2.

31 'Let her weep a little': for the force of по-, see n. to l. 2, and, for the constr., n. to XXV 3.

IV

THE POISON-TREE.

Alexander Púshkin, born at Moscow in 1799, died on Jan. 27, 1837; like Lérmontov, he fell in a duel. Púshkin had African blood in his veins: his mother's grandfather was a negro named Hannibal, who was bought by Peter the Great at Constantinople, educated, and ennobled: the surname borne by his descendants was Ганнибáлъ. There is no trace of the African in Púshkin's writing: apart from his genius, he has the lucidity and good sense of the French people. The creator of modern Russian literature and literary style, Púshkin is ranked by his countrymen as the greatest of all the Russian poets. He wrote a number of poems, some unfinished dramas, a fine tragedy, and a novel in prose. Евгеній Онѣгинъ, a romance in verse, is perhaps his masterpiece; that admirable performance must not be judged by the first Canto which he himself described as 'a hasty introduction.'

This famous poem, a marvel of conciseness and force, may be due to something Púshkin had read about Java; or he may have expanded a hint in Byron's *Childe Harold*, IV 126. One of Turgénev's short novels—Затишье—turns on the poem.

2 рас-калённой: perf. pass. part. from рас-калить: cf. за-калёнъ, V 14.

3 анчáръ: *antiaris* is the botanical name of the upas-tree of Java, a poisonous tree but not quite as deadly as legend represents it.

4 в-селéнная, lit. 'the inhabited,' just like ἡ οἰκουμένη; 'the whole world.'

5 'Nature, the nature of the parched plains.'

жáждущихъ: gen. plur. fem. of the pres. participle of жáждать, 'to thirst.'

степей: gen. plur.: степь generally means a grassy plain, but this tree grows in a sandy desert (l. 20).

6 егó, 'it': Russian uses егó, емý, etc. of animate and inanimate things alike.

въ день, 'upon a day': день is acc.: cf. въ бýрю, 'in a storm' (VII 14).

8 на-поила: here and often the prefix на- suggests abundance:

so на-говори́ть, 'to talk a great deal,' на-пи́ться ча́емъ, 'to drink a quantity of tea.'

9 ка́плетъ: ка́пать, 'to trickle,' makes two presents—ка́паю, —аешь, and ка́плю, —лешь. Note that, if a verb is accented on the 1st syll. in the inf., the accent is unchanged throughout all inflexions.

10 къ полу́дню, 'towards noon': common temporal use of къ.

рас-топя́сь: gerund of the perfective рас-топи́ться, 'to melt.'

зно́ю: the normal gen. of зной is зно́я; but a gen. in -у or -ю is often used, in the case of most masculine nouns: cf. съ ви́ду (v 25).

12 смоло́ю, 'in the form of resin': a typical use of the instrumental case to denote a state or condition: so когда́ я былъ студентомъ, 'when I was a student'; онъ вы́-шелъ въ отста́вку маіо́ромъ, 'he left the army as a major'; онъ смо́тритъ старико́мъ, 'he looks like an old man.'

15 на-бѣжи́тъ: here на- means 'towards,' quite unlike its meaning in на-поила above.

17 е́сли: pronounce *yéss-lee*: Russian с never has the sound of *z*.

о-роси́тъ, lit. 'shall wet': the verb is perfective, and therefore the pres. is future in sense.

18 блуждая: pres. gerund.

19 съ его́ вѣтве́й, 'from its branches': съ with gen. regularly = 'from.' Note that его́, though preceded by a preposition, does not become него́, because the preposition does not govern it: comp. XVI 14.

20 с-тека́етъ: imperfective: the prefix с- means 'from,' like 'ex-' in 'exudes.'

21 'But one human being sent another,' though no wild animal will approach the tree. люди is generally used as the plur. of человѣкъ.

23 тотъ, 'he,' 'the other,' used just like Latin *ille*, where the subject changes.

по-тёкъ (pronounce *pa-tyók*), lit. 'flowed off,' i.e. hastened off.

24 къ у́тру: comp. къ полу́дню (l. 10).

26 у-вя́дшими: past participle of у-вя́нуть, 'to wither.'

съ, 'with,' regularly takes the instr.

28 хла́дный is often used for холо́дный by the poets, and so

власы́ (hair) for во́лосы, младо́й for молодо́й, гласъ for го́лосъ, etc.: in each case the shorter form is the older.

ручья́ми, lit. 'in the form of streams': see n. to l. 12.

29 лёгъ (pronounce *lyok*), past tense of лечь, 'to lie down': all the verbs in this stanza are perfective; each action is definite and complete.

30 лы́ки: the inner bark of a tree, especially the lime, used for many purposes in Russia.

31 ногъ: gen. plur. with what is called the zero ending: i.e. the case represents the stem alone: it is specially common with fem. nouns ending in -a.

33 на-пита́лъ, 'fed to the full': for this force of на-, see n. to l. 8.

34 The epithet means that the arrows do his bidding.

стрѣ́лы in the pl., but стрѣлы́ gen. sing.: see n. to I 2.

35 раз-о-сла́лъ, 'sent in different directions.' The prefix раз- often denotes dispersion; -о- is often inserted between the simple verb and the prefixes воз- and раз-.

36 въ, 'into,' with acc.; but въ, 'in,' takes the loc.

предѣ́лъ, properly 'frontier,' can mean 'country'; Púshkin elsewhere uses родно́й предѣ́лъ for ро́дина (native country).

V.

A COSSACK CRADLE-SONG.

This exquisite song is supposed to be sung by a Cossack woman to her infant. The scene is in the Caucasus, and she foretells that the babe like his father will fight against the mountain tribes, while she weeps at home for her son. The Terek is a great river flowing northwards from the Caucasus, and the Chechens are a tribe living in Daghestan, who resisted the Russian power down to 1859, when they surrendered with their chief, Shamyl.

2 ба́юшки-баю́ is a refrain to make the child sleep, like our 'hush-a-by.' The verb у-баю́кивать = 'to lull to sleep.'

5 ста́ну, 'I will begin' (pres. ind. of стать), is used to form a future tense, 'I will tell': the constr. is common, and it must be noted that the infin. after ста́ну must always be imperfective: there are six such infinitives in the song.

6 с-пою́, 'I will sing': this is the other way of forming the future: с-пою́ is pres. ind. of с-пѣть, and с-пѣть is the perfective form of пѣть: see n. to III 5: this kind of future also occurs six times in the song.

7 жъ = 'but.'

дремли́, imperative of дрема́ть.

за-кры́вши: past gerund of за-кры́ть: the ordinary form is за-кры́въ.

10 плёщетъ: плеска́ть makes плещу́, —ешь, in pres. ind.

11 Чече́нъ: the form Чече́нецъ is commoner: comp. Púshkin, *Prisoner of the Caucasus*,

Не спи, каза́къ: во тмѣ ночно́й
Чече́нецъ хо́дитъ за рѣко́й.

(Sleep not, Cossack; in the darkness of night the Chechen is astir across the river.)

на бе́регъ, 'on to the bank': the acc. shows 'motion to.'

12 то́читъ must be distinguished from точи́ть (inf.).

13 The dash before ста́рый means that 'is' must be supplied: see II 2.

14 за-калёнъ, not being the predicate, should be за-калённый: see n. to III 12: but the distinction between the use of the two forms is sometimes ignored.

въ бою́, 'in battle': the normal locative is бо́ѣ, but many locatives are formed in -у́ or -ю́: so краю́ in l. 38. As this termination is always accented, it is distinct from the dative бо́ю and кра́ю.

15 с-поко́енъ: the short, predicative, form of с-поко́йный.

17 у-зна́ешь, 'thou shalt learn,' from the perfective у-знать: the imperfective is у-знаёшь, 'thou art learning,' from у-знавать.

19 в-дѣ́нешь, 'thou shalt put in,' perfective: but в-дѣва́ешь, 'thou dost put in,' imperfective.

но́гу, acc. of нога́: many fem. nouns which end in а́, throw back the accent in the acc. sing., e.g. рука́, ру́ку, голова́, го́лову.

20 возь-мёшь, 'thou shalt take,' from взять, perfective: but берёшь, 'thou art taking,' from брать, imperfective.

22 раз-о-шью́, 'I will embroider': but рас-шива́ю, 'I embroider.' The prefix раз- (of which рас- and разо- are other forms) suggests variety, 'divers colours.'

25 съ виду, 'in appearance,' lit. 'from look': for the -у ending

of the gen., see n. to IV 10: so терять изъ виду, 'to lose sight of.'

27 я выйду, 'I will go out': вы- is always accented, when the verb to which it is prefixed is perfective; so вы-слала (I 8).

28 ты махнёшь, 'thou wilt beckon,' from махнуть: but машешь, 'thou beckonest,' from махать.

29 слёзъ: gen. plur. with zero ending, governed by сколько.

30 въ ту ночь, 'on that night': ту is fem. acc. of тотъ.

про-лью, 'I shall shed,' from про-лить: but лью, 'I am shedding.'

33 стану: see l. 5: five impertective infinitives here follow the auxiliary verb.

35 цѣлый день: acc. of duration of time.

36 гадать, to discover her son's destiny by cards or by omens; гаданіе was a favourite pastime of Russian women in the days of their ignorance.

37 скучаешь, sc. по родинѣ, 'art homesick.'

38 краю: see n. to l. 14.

39 жъ = 'but.'

заботъ: gen. plur. with zero ending, from забота: the gen. is used because the verb is negatived: see n. to III 30.

41 дамъ, 'I will give,' from дать: but даю, 'I give,' from the imperfective давать.

She will give him at parting a little *ikon*, to which he may address his prayers.

A Russian peasant, when praying, turns his eyes to the sacred pictures (образа) on the house-wall. If out of doors, he will look, if possible, at the cross on a church, and is said молиться Богу на церковный крестъ, i.e. 'to direct prayer to the church cross.'

43 молясь-я: the proper gerund of молиться (to pray) is молясь, but the poets often add a superfluous -а or -я to the reflexive verb.

44 ставь, imperative of ставить.

передъ собой, 'in front of you': себя and свой (l. 46) are freely used of the 1st and 2nd persons, as well as of the 3rd: e.g. я позволю себѣ прибавить, 'I shall permit myself to add....'

45 готовясь: pres. gerund of готовиться.

въ бой, 'to enter the battle.'

46 помни: imperative of помнить: the accent, being on the first syll. in the inf., remains there in all the inflexions.

VI.

ERZERUM.

This poem was written at Erzerum, which Púshkin visited in 1829; Russia was at war with Turkey, and Púshkin entered the city with a victorious army. The poem, attributed to a Turkish Janissary, appeared in an account of the journey which he published. In this he writes: 'The reforms instituted by the Sultan have not yet penetrated to Erzerum. Between Erzerum and Constantinople there exists the same sort of rivalry as between Kazan and Moscow.'

1 гяу́ры, 'the Giaours,' i.e. the Christian powers who complimented the Sultan Mahmoud on his reforms.

2 ко́ваной пято́й, 'with iron heel': кова́ть, 'to hammer iron,' makes кую́, куёшь, in pres. ind.; and ко́ванный, the perf. pass. part., is used as an adj. with one н dropped out.

3 спя́щаго: acc. sing. masc., pres. part. of спать.

раз-да́вятъ and the two following verbs, being perfectives, are all future in meaning.

5 за-сну́лъ, 'has fallen asleep': про-сну́ть-ся, 'to awake,' is a reflexive verb: both are perfectives.

6 Про-ро́ка, 'the Prophet,' Mahomet.

7 въ нёмъ, 'in it': pronounce *vnyom* (1 syll.).

дре́вняго: most adjectives of time and place have 'soft' terminations: e.g. весенній (not —ый), лѣтній, зи́мній, ра́нній, пре́жній, послѣдній, вече́рній, which are all found in this text.

9 'For the sweets of vice': сла́достей is gen. plur. and governs поро́ка.

10 мольбѣ: из-мѣни́ть, 'to betray,' governs the dat.

11 от-вы́къ, 'has become unaccustomed': but при-вы́къ, 'has become accustomed.'

по́ту: for gen. in -у, see n. to IV 10: distinguish this from въ поту́, 'in a sweat,' where the loc. ending is accented.

12 въ часы́, 'at the hours.'

14 хо́дятъ, 'walk on foot': the verb further implies that they do this as a regular thing, whereas иду́тъ would mean 'they are walking now': cf. XIII 5: ходи́ть and идти́ are both imperfectives, so that their presents have a present sense; but the

first is 'indefinite' and the second 'definite.' Thus ру́сскій мужи́къ ка́ждую суббо́ту хо́дитъ въ ба́ню, 'a Russian peasant goes to the bath every Saturday'; but онъ идётъ въ ба́ню, 'he is going to the bath now.' Compounds of ходи́ть are imperfective, but of идти́ perfective: hence про-хо́дитъ = 'he walks forward,' but про-йдётъ = 'he will go,' the prefix losing its proper meaning, and serving only to make the verb perfective: see Appendix I § 5.

Note the change of accent between ходи́ть (inf.) and хо́дитъ, 'he walks.'

15 стару́хъ, like мужчи́нъ below, is acc. plur., this case being identical with the gen. if the noun is animate. But note that the acc. *sing.* of fem. nouns in -a differs from the gen. sing.

16 а тѣ: comp. и тотъ (IV 23).

гаре́мы, 'the harems': Púshkin first wrote харе́мы, which reproduces the sound of *h* better; but modern Russian always uses г to represent our *h*, so that Hamlet is turned into Гамле́тъ and Horatio into Гора́цій.

в-во́дятъ: the prefix means 'into': it does not form a syllable and is pronounced as if the speaker had a very slight stammer over the letter.

17 евну́хъ: pronounce *yev-noóch* (*ch* as in loch).

18 не тако́въ, '[is] not like that.'

The epithets refer to the facts that Erzerum is (1) 7000 feet above the sea; (2) a centre of trade-routes between Europe and Asia. This appears in Púshkin's prose narrative.

21 че́рплемъ: the regular form from че́рпать, 'to draw,' is че́рпаемъ.

ча́шей: instrumental.

24 Púshkin writes: 'Erzerum is proud of its water. The Euphrates flows within three *versts* of the town; and there are everywhere a quantity of fountains, with a tin cup by each, hanging on a chain.'

25 толпо́й: for this use of the instr., see n. to IV 12.

26 джиги́ты: a Tatar word: no Russian word begins with дж-: they use it to represent our *j* sound, e.g. дже́нтельменъ, 'gentleman'; Джемсъ, 'James.'

28 As a matter of fact, Púshkin describes in his narrative how he himself visited a harem at Erzerum; but the visit was made by right of conquest.

VII.

THE AMULET.

This imitation of Eastern poetry is based on fact. At Odessa in 1824, Púshkin was given an agate seal-ring by a Countess Vorontsoff. He wore it habitually on his right thumb—some of his portraits show it—often used it to seal his letters, and attached a mysterious value to it. It was once in the possession of Turgénev, and is now in the Púshkin Museum at Petrograd. It bears a memorial inscription in Hebrew, but is not of great antiquity.

2 на, 'against.'

скалы́, acc. plur.: an exception to the rule noted on I 2.

3 тёпло, 'warmly,' makes теплѣ́е as comparative: where the positive has more than two syllables, the accent does not shift in the comp., e.g. учти́во, 'politely,' makes учти́вѣе.

5 на-слажда́-я-сь: pres. gerund of the imperfective на-слажда́ться: note that perfective verbs do not normally form pres. gerunds.

The termination -сь, after vowels, represents the termination -ся (pronounced *-sa*) after consonants.

6 про-во́дитъ, 'spends'; but the other aspect про-ведётъ would mean 'will spend.'

7 ласка́ясь: the reflexive form implies that the endearments are mutual.

8 в-ручи́ла = the Latin *mandavit*, being derived from рука́ as *mandare* is from *manus*.

12 'It [is] given to you by love.' The instr. is constantly used to express agency: cf. XIV 28.

данъ is the passive participle used as predicate and therefore in the short form: the two forms are да́нный, —ая, —ое, and данъ, дана́, дано́, where the shift of accent should be noted.

15 головы́: gen., because the verb governing it is negative: the pl. is го́ловы, the same form with a different accent.

16 спасётъ and the three following verbs are all perfective presents with future meaning.

19 по-кло́нниковъ is the form of both gen. and acc.; but the gen. is no doubt required here by the negative verb.

Про-ро́ка: cf. VI 6.

21 на, 'to.'

ло́но, a poetical word, for which ру́ки or грудь would be used in prose.

22 странъ: gen. plur. with zero ending, from страна́.

23 съ ю́га, 'from the South': pronounce *syooga*: newspapers now write of the Southern Slavs as Jugo-Slavs.

25 кова́рны should be кова́рныя: see n. to III 12: but the poets often disregard the difference: comp. XIX 5.

о́чи, a poetical word, for which глаза́ is used in prose: the sing. is о́ко, —a, n.

26 очару́ютъ: from очарова́ть: future in sense. An inf. in -ова́ть generally makes a pres. ind. in -у́ю, -у́ешь.

27 уста́: the prose equivalent is гу́бы.

28 поцѣлу́ютъ: another perfective.

любя́: gerund of люби́ть.

31 отъ забве́нья, 'from being forgotten.'

32 со-храни́тъ, 'will preserve': but храни́тъ, 'preserves,' and храни́ть, 'to preserve.'

VIII.

A SERENADE.

Iván Turgénev (1818–1883) is of all Russian writers the finest artist and the best critic. The amount of his prose fiction is very large, and it is all good; one might pick out Запи́ски Охо́тника, Отцы́ и Дѣ́ти, and Ру́динъ (*A Sportsman's Notes*, *Fathers and Sons*, *Rúdin*), as his masterpieces. He published little poetry; the single piece (*Croquet at Windsor*) which he included in the collected edition of his works, is unworthy of him.

This graceful and musical serenade is taken from his earliest piece for the stage, called Неосторо́жность (*Carelessness*), written in 1843. The scene is in Spain.

2 подъ окно́мъ, 'under the window,' the speaker being in the street: a person is often said сидѣ́ть подъ окно́мъ, when he is in the house: cf. XVIII 6.

за-вѣ́шеннымъ: past pass. part. of за-вѣ́сить: a theatre curtain is за́-на-вѣсъ.

3 тѣни́: locative, to be distinguished from тѣ́ни, gen. and dat. sing., nom. and acc. pl., of the same word. This loc. is

found in fem. nouns ending either in -ь, like тѣнь, or in -ія, like А́нглія; въ А́нгліи, 'in England.'

4 о-ку́танный, 'wrapped about': the prefix о- often has this force.

5 звѣ́зды: pronounce звёзды: this is one of a very few words in which ѣ takes this sound which е so often has.

7 вы́йдь is one syllable: the imperative of the imperfective is вы-ходи́: the latter would be a less urgent summons.

8 по-яви́-сь, 'show thyself': the -сь represents -ся, i.e. себя́.

9 'However long we may live after this.'

ни is not negative here: after an interrogative-relative adverb or pronoun, it expresses the indefinite notion of 'however': e.g. какъ я ни стара́юсь, 'however hard I try.'

When бы is also used, as here, the verb is always in the past: comp. III 10 кто бы ни спроси́лъ; XXV 2 кто бъ ты ни́ былъ: бъ is the contracted form of бы.

10 хотѣ́ть, 'to wish,' an irregular verb, makes хочу́, хо́чешь, хо́четъ, хоти́мъ, хоти́те, хотя́тъ.

чтобъ = что бы, and this again is followed by a past tense where we should expect a present.

мы съ тобо́й = 'you and I': the regular idiom, the speaker putting himself first, in the plural: 'my sister and I' is мы съ сестро́й.

12 но́чи: gen., as the object of a negatived verb.

13 легко́, ле́гче, 'lightly': adv. of лёгкій.

14 дыша́: gerund of дыша́ть.

15 о-зира́ясь, 'looking about you': gerund of о-зира́ться.

16 ты сойдёшь, 'thou wilt come down,' perfective: с-хо́дишь, the imperfective, 'thou art coming down.'

душа́: often used as a term of endearment, even between men.

17 торжеству́я: gerund of торжествова́ть: observe how much commoner the gerund is than the present participle.

18–23 All the verbs are perfective presents with future meaning.

18 крыльцо́ = French *perron*, steps outside a house: a Russian family in summer spends much time на крыльцѣ́.

19 колѣ́ни, irregular pl. from колѣ́но.

у-паду́, from у-па́сть: the imperfective is па́даю.

20 тебѣ въ лицо́, 'into your face'; the regular idiom.

21 The imperfectives of the three verbs are—за-тиха́етъ, про-хо́дитъ, and за-мира́етъ.

24 пре-дáвшихся, lit. 'that have surrendered themselves': past part. of the reflexive verb пре-дáть-ся.

25 с-ложи́вши рýки, lit. 'having folded your arms': past gerund of с-ложить. All gerunds are indeclinable.

The three finite verbs in this stanza are imperfectives.

26 объ becomes óбо before мн-, just as къ becomes ко (l. 16) and въ becomes во.

27 лью́тся: pronounce *léwtsa*: Newton's name is written Нью́тонъ in Russian.

IX.

A SONG.

Alexéi Koltsóv (1809–1842) had a short and sad life. The son of a cattle-dealer in the Government of Voronezh, he received little education and found no sympathy nor even affection in his own family. His chief friend and patron was the critic Byelínsky. After long illness he died of consumption, leaving 158 short poems. There is much resemblance between his history and that of Burns. He had an admirable lyric gift, and more of his songs would have been included here, if his metres, often those of the traditional folk-songs, had been more suitable to the immediate purpose of the book.

The metre is ◡ ◡ ⏊ | ◡ ◡ ⏊, i.e. two anapaests, with the last syll. of each foot accented.

2 жарче, 'more hotly,' comp. of жáрко: for the form, comp. пýще (xv 12).

дня: 'than' after the comparative is regularly expressed by the gen.: э́то вы лýчше меня́ знáете, 'you know that better than I.'

3 With a personal dat., the inf. is freely used to express negations: comp. xi 2: 'we cannot tell' may be either не намъ знать or какъ намъ знать?

други́мъ: dat. plur. of другóй.

6 жилá: the past tense of the Russian verb has the peculiarity of showing gender and number—онъ жилъ, онá жилá, онó жило, они жили. This is explained by the fact that it was once a participle; thus it is analogous to the Latin passive, *captus est, capta est, capti sunt*. The fem. form is apt to place the accent on the last syllable: so от-дала below.

7 дýшу, acc. of душá, with change of accent: see n. to v 19.

8 от-дала́: but о́т-далъ where the subject is masculine. от-дала́ and по-гаси́ (l. 17) are the only perfectives in the poem, as against fourteen imperfectives.

9 что за ночь = кака́я ночь, 'what a wonderful night': comp. XXII 1. Note that in this idiom за does not affect the case of the noun which follows it.

10 дру́га: verbs of expecting govern the gen.
другъ, дру́га must not be confused with друго́й, друго́го (l. 3).

11 The masc. forms are блѣденъ and хо́лоденъ, being the contracted forms; but the fem. forms, in these and many other cases, accent the last syllable.

13 поётъ: пѣть, 'to sing,' makes пою́, поёшь etc.

14 зо́рька, dim. of заря́, 'redness of the sky,' is used as an endearment: so also is со́лнышко, dim. of со́лнце.

15 берётъ, 'he takes,' from бра́ть: but возьмётъ, 'he will take,' from взять: the perfective is therefore supplied by a quite different verb.

17 по-гаси́: perfective imperative: по-гаша́й imperfective.

18 по-цѣлу́и, a pl. noun of four syllables, must not be confused with по-цѣлу́й, an imperative of three.

20 огнь: a contracted form of ого́нь.
въ крови́: loc., but the gen. of кровь is кро́ви.

22 жжётъ: жечь, 'to burn,' makes жгу, жжёшь etc.

X.

THE SCENT OF THE BIRCH-TREE.

Alexéi Tolstói (1817–1875)—not nearly related, if at all, to the more famous writer of the same name—had all the advantages of birth and wealth. For twenty years he held a position at Court, corresponding to that of Master of the Buckhounds. But literature was the chief passion of his whole life; and he left a trilogy of historical dramas, a historical novel of the time of Ivan the Terrible, and a quantity of lyric poetry, including epical ballads such as no Russian had written before him. His lyrics seem to show the influence of Heine. All his published writings are excellent literature; and his plays are successful on the stage.

This lovely little poem has an exquisite freshness which is rare in any poetry.

I веснóй, 'in spring': see n. to I 2.

2 вс-ходи́ла, 'was rising up': the prefix воз- (вос- and вс- are forms of it) denotes upward motion.

3 текли́: the past tense of течь, 'to flow,' is тёкъ, текла́, текло́, текли́.

4 рощъ: gen. plur., with zero ending, of рóща.

5 пасту́шья, belonging to a пасту́хъ, 'herdsman.' It was still too early in spring for the sheep and cattle to be driven out to pasture: the grass had not grown tall enough.

7 въ завиткáхъ былъ, 'was in curls,' i.e. was still curled up in the frond.

въ бору́: for the loc. ending in -у́ or -ю́, see n. to V 14.

10 берёзъ: gen. plur. with zero ending.

11 предъ (= пéредъ) becomes прéдо before мн-, as объ becomes óбо (III 27).

13 то, 'then.'

на is governed by отвѣ́тъ—'in answer to.'

15 сóлнца: in this word the л is generally not pronounced.

18 гля́дя: as the inf. is глядѣть, the normal gerund would be глядя́, but there are a few gerunds which throw back the accent, e.g. гля́дя, стóя, си́дя, лёжа.

22 счáстіе and счáстье are equally permissible spellings; but the latter, having only two syllables, would not fit the verse here.

XI.

DEATH.

This is the end of a long poem by Lérmontov, called *Mtsyri* or *The Novice.* A Georgian boy who had been brought up in a Russian monastery escaped to the freedom of his native mountains and returned, after a few days, brought to the point of death by exhaustion and want of food. Nearly all the poem is spoken by him: he tells the Abbot why he went and what he did, and ends with this charge about his last hours.

I стáну у-мирáть, 'shall come to die.'

стáну, itself perfective, is constantly used with imperfective infinitives to form a future: see Appendix I § 9.

2 вѣрь, вѣрьте, imperative of вѣ́рить.

тебѣ—ждать, 'you will not have long to wait': see n. to IX 3.

3 пере-нéсть: the prefix has the same force as 'trans-' in 'transport': it signifies a change of place.

несть is another form of нестú.

велú: imperative of велѣ́ть. Note that велю́ belongs to both aspects, perfective and imperfective, and means (1) 'I will order'; (2) 'I order.' The number of such verbs is small.

4 то, 'that,' not 'the.'

цвѣлú: 'used to bloom': 3rd plur., past tense of цвѣстú.

5 акáцій: gen. plur.: not to be confused with акáціи loc. sing., which has four syllables, not three.

два кустá: a substantive following два, три, or четы́ре must be in the gen. sing., e.g. два старикá, 'two old men'; двѣ сестры́, 'two sisters': for the origin of this singular idiom, see Forbes, p. 91.

6 такъ густá, '[is] so thick': такъ can be used thus with the short form of an adjective, but такъ густáя травá would be impossible, такóй, такáя being always used with the long form of the adj. So 'what a fine man!' is какóй слáвный человѣ́къ, and never какъ слáвный. See XXII 2.

7 The l. illustrates the convenience, or rather necessity, of the double form of the adjective where *is* is not expressed: свѣ́жій, being a long form, must be an epithet of the noun; душúстъ, being a short form, must be the predicate.

9 игрáющій: pres. participle of игрáть.

листъ, 'foliage.'

10 по-ложúть, 'to lay,' is the perfective of класть, while ложúться is itself the imperfective of лечь, 'to lie.'

Observe the accent and meaning of the common phrase по-лóжимъ, 'let us suppose.'

11 голубáго: pronounce *galubáwva*: голубóи, derived from гóлубь, 'a pigeon,' means 'pigeon-coloured,' as distinct from сúній, 'dark blue.'

12 у-пью́с-я, 'I will intoxicate myself': a perfective compound of пить, 'to drink.' For the termination, see n. to v 43.

разъ: pronounce *rass*.

13 вúденъ, the short form of вúдный.

14 съ, 'from,' coalesces wholly with the following word.

15 при-шлётъ, 'will send,' from при-слáть: the imperfective is при-сылáть.

18 роднóй звукъ, 'the dear native sound' of the mountain breeze: the adj. implies both ideas.

раз-дáст-ся, 'will be heard'; but раз-даёт-ся, 'is being heard.'

20 с-клонѝвшись: past gerund.

21 о-тёръ, fem. о-тёрла: past tense of о-терéть. All compounds of тереть are perfective, all of тирáть are imperfective.

съ is not required, as the instr. alone would give the same meaning.

22 кончѝны: gen. governed by потъ.

хлáдный: see n. to IV 28.

23 въ пол-гóлоса, lit. 'in half a voice': гóлоса is gen. governed by пол-.

поётъ: cf. IX 13.

24 про, 'about': with the same meaning as о, объ.

25 за-сну́: cf. VI 5.

26 про-кляну́, 'I will curse': про-кля́сть makes про-кляну́, —нёшь etc.: the imperfective, про-клинáть, makes про-клинáю.

The dying boy means that, but for this last consolation, he must have cursed the Russian monks who had kept him shut up in the monastery.

XII.

ON A DEATH-BED.

A fine example of the skill with which Tyúchev fits a scene of intense human feeling into a frame of natural scenery perfectly described.

1 весь день: acc.: cf. цѣ́лый день (v 35).

лежáла, 'was lying': this verb and the next three are imperfectives: this aspect, like the imperfect in Greek and Latin, has a dramatic and descriptive force.

за-бытьѝ, loc. of за-бы́тіе: the alternative form, за-бы́тье, makes loc. за-бы́тьѣ.

2 её: pronounce *ye-yó.*

тѣ́ни, the shades of evening.

по-крывáли, 'were covering': по-кры́ли, perfective, would mean 'covered,' or 'have covered,' or 'had covered.'

3 лѣ́тній: for the soft terminations of these adjectives, see n. to VI 7.

4 ли́стьямъ: листъ has two plurals: (1) ли́стья, —ьевъ, 'foliage'; (2) листы́, —о́въ, 'leaves' of books etc.

6 начала́: but на́чалъ, '*he* began.'

This verb, and its imperfective начина́ть, are always followed by imperfective infinitives.

7 слу́шала, 'went on listening,' imperfective.

у-влечена́ and по-гружена́ are short forms of passive participles: the long forms are у-влечённая (from у-влечь) and по-гружённая (from по-грузи́ть); both are perfectives.

8 ду́му, 'a thought': the same word denotes a deliberative body: городская ду́ма, 'a town-council': the Russian House of Commons is called the Dúma, and is pronounced *Doó-ma.*

9 какъ бы, 'as if': there are many equivalent expressions—какъ бу́дто, бу́дто, сло́вно etc.

бесѣ́дуя: pres. gerund of бесѣ́довать.

10 про-говори́ла, 'articulated': the prefix про- suggests that she had difficulty in bringing out the words.

11 у-битый is past part. pass. of у-би́ть, 'to kill,' but can mean less than 'killed': до сме́рти, 'to death,' is often added to the verb, to make the meaning precise.

12 всё э́то, i.e. the pattering of the summer rain on the leaves, and Nature in general.

люби́ла, 'used to love': imperfective.

13–16 Yes, says the poet; your power of loving was such as no one ever possessed before; and yet I was able to survive your death!

14 у-два́ться is an impersonal verb, used with the dative: не зна́ю, уда́стся-ли мнѣ, 'I do not know whether I shall be successful'; тебѣ́ удало́сь, 'thou wert successful'; ему́ у-даётся, 'he is successful.'

у-дава́лось is imperfective: note that negative and interrogative sentences tend to use imperfective rather than perfective in the past tense: see Appendix I § 11.

15 Го́споди: voc. of Госпо́дь: one of the few vocatives preserved in the language; Бо́же, 'O God,' from Богъ, is another.

и э́то пере-жи́ть, 'to survive even this!' We should not use the infinitive quite in this way.

Note that жить, 'to live,' imperfective and intransitive, becomes, when compounded with пере-, both perfective and transitive—'to outlive.'

16 раз-о-рва́лось: раз- = 'asunder,' and рвать, 'to tear,' when compounded with раз-, becomes perfective, with раз-рыва́ть as its imperfective.

XIII.

THE CONVICTS.

A party of convicts, moving in chains along the dusty high-road, strike up a song to raise their spirits, and the subject of their singing is the life of freedom on the wide steppes and great rivers of Russia. Alexéi Tolstói is admirably skilful in describing scenes of the road: see XIV and XXII.

The metre is Heine's ballad-metre, with three beats:

Du hást Diamánten und Pérlen,
Hast Álles, was Ménschenbegéhr.

The third l. sometimes rhymes with the first, and sometimes not.

1 с-пуска́ется, 'is sinking': but с-пу́стится, 'will sink.' Note that all compounds of пуска́ть are imperfective, and all compounds of пусти́ть perfective.

за сте́пи: за, 'behind,' here takes acc. because the sun is moving: for за with instr., see XXI 22.

2 вдали́, adv., is for въ дали́, 'in the distance,' from даль. The setting sun gilds the grass.

4 вз-мета́ютъ, 'stir up': the prefix, a form of воз-, means 'upwards.' The men wear chains (кандалы́) on their legs.

Distinguish пыль, —и, f. 'dust,' from пылъ, 'flame.'

5 иду́тъ, 'they are walking': see n. to хо́дятъ (VI 14).

бри́тый is pass. part. of брить, 'to shave.'

лба́ми: лобъ, gen. лба; so ротъ, 'mouth,' gen. рта: во лбу, 'on the forehead,' во рту, 'in the mouth.' The shaven fore-head was in old days a mark, not only of the convict but of the newly-enrolled recruit in the Army.

7 с-дви́нули, 'they have moved close,' i.e. knitted: perfective.

8 The past tense of лечь is лёгъ, легла́, —о́, —и́; also perfective.

9 тѣ́ни, i.e. their own shadows.

10 кля́чи: gen. sing.: see n. to XI 5.

везу́тъ: везти́, 'to carry (on wheels),' makes везу́, везёшь etc.: 'to carry in your hand or arms' is нести́.

11 с-гибáя, pres. gerund of с-гибáть which has со-гнýть as perfective.

12 идýтъ shows that the guards are on foot too: the cart conveys necessaries for the party.

13 что = 'well,' 'I say.'

за-тя́немте, 'let us strike up': за-тя́немъ, 1st pers. pl., pres. tense of the perfective за-тянýть, can bear this meaning of itself, but -те is often added to a verb so used: 'let us go' may be expressed either by по-йдёмъ, or by по-йдём-те. Thus за-бýдемъ below = 'let us forget.'

15 ужъ, contracted form of ужé: one of the commonest words in conversation, with the meaning 'certainly': ужé more often means 'already'; but both forms can have either meaning. Note that ýже (so accented) is 'more narrowly.'

16 на-пи́сана is predicate, and the verb былá is not expressed.

на родý, 'at birth': for the loc. in -ý, see n. to v 14. The convicts console themselves by reflecting that they cannot escape their destiny. So when the old miller was drowned in Aksakov's *Childhood*, the maids say, ужъ емý такъ на родý напи́сано (p. 220).

17 по-вели́, 'they started off,' from по-води́ть.

18 пою́тъ: from пѣть.

за-ливáть-ся, a reflexive compound of -ливáть, 'to pour,' is often said of singers using loud and high notes. Cf. за-ливáть-ся смѣ́хомъ, 'to laugh heartily,' and за-ливáть-ся слезáми, 'to weep copiously.'

19 про: see n. to XI 24.

широ́кой: in poetry the adj. often follows the noun.

20 дáромъ, originally the instr. of даръ 'a gift,' is used as an adverb, meaning 'as a gift,' 'for nothing,' 'with nothing to show for it': see XV 1.

минýвшiе: past part. act. of минýть.

22 ди́кую во́лю, 'the freedom of the wild'; во́ля means (1) freedom, (2) control.

23 всё: here an adv.

цѣ́пи: nom. plur.

24 метýтъ: мести́, 'to sweep,' makes метý, метёшь etc.

XIV.

A PICTURE OF TRAVEL.

This poem, like the last, describes a Russian landscape and figures seen by a traveller—a weir, a lake, and a mill, peasants sitting on the grass, a Jew walking over the weir, a boy in the reed-bed; and the traveller has the sensation that he saw all this once before.

For Mr Baring's translation of this poem, see Appendix II.

2 рыба́чій, an adj. from рыба́къ, 'a fisherman': so пасту́шій from пасту́хъ (x 5).

3 ѣ́детъ (from ѣ́хать), and not идётъ, is said of the carriage as well as of the persons conveyed in it: comp. I 6.

4 ней: loc., with н prefixed owing to the preposition: as the loc. is only used after prepositions, ней and нёмъ are the only forms found.

5 доро́гой, 'on the way': дорого́й is an adj., meaning 'dear.'

8 деревня does not have the zero ending, дере́внь, for its gen. plur., but inserts a vowel after the в.

10 про-хо́дитъ: see n. to VI 14.

из-о́-рванный, 'ragged,' is originally past part. passive of из-о-рва́ть (with imperfective из-рыва́ть), 'to tear in pieces.'

жидъ: rather an offensive word for a Jew, who is more politely spoken of as евре́й, 'a Hebrew.'

13 Note the idiom игра́ть на ду́дкѣ of a musical instrument but игра́ть въ ка́рты, 'to play at cards,' and игра́ть въ ку́клы, 'to play with dolls.'

14 за-бра́вши-сь: past gerund of за-бра́ться.

15 вз-летѣ́вшія: nom. pl. fem., past part. act. of вз-летѣ́ть: for the meaning of the prefix вз-, see n. to XIII 4.

16 по́дняли, 'have raised': perfective: comp. XV 8.

20 под-во́зитъ, 'carries up': distinguished from the inf. под-вози́ть by accent and final letter: imperfective, as the meaning shows; the perfective is под-везти́.

21 ка́жется: каза́ться, 'to seem,' from which this comes, must not be confused with каса́ться, 'to touch,' e.g. что до меня́ каса́ется, 'so far as I am concerned.'

22 хоть: contracted form of хотя́, which was once the pres. gerund of хотѣ́ть, 'to wish,' but has now become a conjunction meaning 'although.'

нé is accented, because былъ and было́ (but not была́) throw back their accent when they follow не.

25 го́воръ, lit. 'talking': a noun formed from говори́ть.

26 гумно́ is a stack-yard with a threshing-floor in it.

27 когда́-то, 'some time or other': то, tacked on to кто, что, какъ, гдѣ, когда́ etc., serves to make the pronoun or adv. indefinite.

ужъ, 'already,' here.

28 мно́ю, 'by me': for this use of the instr. to express agency, see VII 12.

29 ступа́ла, 'was walking': uncompleted actions are described, and the imperfective is therefore needed; the four following verbs are all past imperfectives.

30 такі́е-жъ, 'just the same': comp. та́кже, 'also.'

33 шёлъ, 'was walking,' irregular past of идти́, with fem. шла and pl. шли.

ходи́лъ, also imperfective, would mean 'used to walk': see n. to VI 14.

XV.

SPRING.

Perhaps this is the best of Tyúchev's spring songs, perfect alike in fancy, form, and music. Landor, in his happiest moments, might have written something like it.

1 зима́, but зи́му (l. 6): see n. to V 19.

не да́ромъ, 'not for nothing,' i.e. with good reason: see n. to XIII 20.

2 'Her time has passed away.'

про-шла́ must not be confused with при-шла́ which has the opposite meaning, 'has come': э́та болѣ́знь ско́ро про-йдётъ, 'that illness will soon pass.'

ея́ (pronounce *ye-yó*): gen. of она́.

пора́ generally means a point of time, and вре́мя a period: мнѣ́ пора́, 'I must be going': but пора́ here means a period.

3 въ окно́, 'at the window.'

стучи́тся: there is little difference in meaning between стуча́ть-ся, the reflexive form of this verb, and the simple form стуча́ть.

4 го́нитъ: гнать, 'to chase,' makes гоню́, го́нишь etc.: note the shift of accent: see n. to I 3.

со двора́ = 'away': lit. 'from the court-yard'; but дворъ loses its original sense in this phrase and in на дворѣ́, 'out of doors' (XXIII 1).

5 всё: a noun here and subject of the verbs.

6 вонъ, 'out': an adv. like Latin *foras*: not to be confused with вонь, —и, f., 'an evil smell.'

8 тре-зво́нъ, properly 'a peal of three or more bells'; hence 'joy-bells' generally: звонъ is the sound made by church-bells, and зво́нкій is 'bell-like,' 'ringing.'

9 хлопота́ть makes хлопочу́, хлопо́чешь etc.; and хохота́ть is inflected in the same way in pres. ind

11 та, 'the other,' i.e. spring: comp. тотъ (IV 23).

ей въ глаза́, 'into her face': cf. VIII 20 тебѣ́ въ лицо́.

12 пу́ще, 'more': пре́жняго, 'than before,' is often added: this adv. has no positive, other than мно́го.

13 вз-бѣси́лась: the prefix вз- turns бѣси́ть-ся into a perfective. For the meaning, comp. бѣсъ, 'the devil,' бѣ́шенство, 'fury' etc.

зла́я, 'ill-natured': fem. of злой.

14 снѣ́гу, 'some snow': the gen. in -у is especially common in this partitive sense: e.g. кусо́чекъ са́хару, 'a lump of sugar.'

за-хватя́ is a pres. gerund, formed from the perfective verb за-хвати́ть: such gerunds are always past in meaning, e.g. у-ви́дя, 'having seen'; but it is exceptional for a perfective verb to form a present gerund at all (Forbes, p. 199).

15 пусти́ла, 'let fly': past perfective, with пуска́ла for imperfective.

Though most perfective verbs are compound, being made perfective by the addition of по- or some other prefix to the simple verb, a certain number are simple: пусти́ть is one of these. Therefore пу́ститъ = 'he will let go,' and пуска́етъ, 'he lets go.' Other simple perfectives found in these poems are стать, 'to begin,' and дать, 'to give.'

у-бѣга́я, 'while running away': pres. gerund of у-бѣга́ть which has as perfective у-бѣжать.

17 'Spring does not care': lit. 'to spring there is even little of distress': го́ря ма́ло is often used thus in prose after a dat. of the person.

18 у-мы́лас-я, 'she washed her face and hands': у-мыва́ть-ся (perfective у-мы́ть-ся) does not mean 'to take a bath,' which is купа́ть-ся.

For the superfluous -я added to the reflexive verb, see n. to v 43.

снѣгу́, loc., but снѣ́гу, gen. (l. 14), and also снѣ́гу, dat.

19 румя́нѣй, 'more ruddy': in the predicate, the comparative of the adv. is regularly used for that of the adj.: e.g. я тогда́ моло́же, я лу́чше, ка́жется, была́, 'I was younger then, I was probably prettier.'

The normal termination of the comp. adv. is -ѣе, but the poets use -ѣй freely when they want one syllable and not two.

20 врагу́: dat.: 'in defiance *to*' is the Russian idiom.

XVI.

THE FIRST LEAVES.

A description of one of the fairest sights the year offers—the 'mist of green' with which trees are veiled in spring; the poet calls the young leaves the 'living dreams' of the trees which now have come to light with the first blue sky; and he ends with the striking thought, that here there is life only with no admixture of death.

1 листъ: collective here, 'the foliage.'

2 ли́стьемъ: instr. of ли́стье, —ья.

3 об-вѣ́яны, 'fanned': the leaves are in motion: comp. вѣ́ять хлѣбъ, 'to winnow corn'; вѣ́еръ, 'a fan.'

4 зе́ленью, instr. of зе́лень, 'verdure'; in apposition with ли́стьемъ.

сквозно́й: comp. x 4.

6 давно́, 'long ago': but не-да́вно, 'not long ago' (see xvii 5), with a change of accent.

имъ гре́зилось весно́й, 'they dreamt of spring': the verb is impersonal and takes an instr. of the thing dreamt of.

10 про-би́лись, 'have pierced through,' perfective: the verb is suited, not to dreams but to the leaves which are identified with them.

на, 'into.'

12 о-мы́тыхъ: gen. plur., past part. passive of о-мы́ть.

14 по ихъ движе́нью, 'by their motion': по with dat. often = 'by means of.'

Note that ихъ, not being governed by по, does not change to нихъ: see IV 19.

15 тьмахъ, 'tens of thousands': this is clearly the meaning here, as it is in Biblical language; but тьма, like 'myriad,' has now come to stand for 'a multitude.' 'A million emeralds break from the ruby-budded lime'—thus Tennyson describes the same sight.

16 не встрѣ́тишь, 'one will not meet': for this use of the 2nd pers. sing. in a generalising sense, see III 26.

The verb being negatived, its direct object листа́ is in the genitive.

XVII.

THE CLOUD.

Turgénev, discussing the different ways in which poets describe nature, says of Púshkin, that his descriptions are never morbid but as simple and natural as an ancient Greek's. 'Who does not know his "Cloud"? But I shall not deny myself the pleasure of copying out the whole of it.' He then does so, underlining for their special excellence ll. 3, 4, 7, 8, 12; and adds the comment, 'Marvellous!' (Vol. X p. 414).

The metre is anapaestic, with four beats:

⏑ ⏑́ | ⏑ ⏑ ⏑́ | ⏑ ⏑ ⏑́ | ⏑ ⏑ ⏑́ | ⏑

1 послѣ́дняя: for the soft termination, see n. to VI 7.

раз-сѣ́янной; lit. 'sown broadcast,' i.e. dispersed. The prefix раз- of itself implies separation.

2 несёшься, 'carriest thyself,' i.e. art borne.

лазу́ри, dat. of лазу́рь, по having its common local sense of 'through,' 'along.'

4 лику́ющій: pres. part. of ликова́ть, which makes лику́ю, —у́ешь: see n. to VII 26.

5 круго́мъ is the instr. of a noun, used as an adv.: comp. да́ромъ (XIII 20).

об-лега́ла: all the verbs in this stanza are past imperfectives.

7 громъ: a compound of this word, по-гро́мъ, 'a riot,' directed especially against the Jews, has found its way into English dictionaries.

8 зéмлю, acc. of землѝ: for the shift of accent, see n. to v 19.
пойла: the perfective of this verb occurred IV 8.

9 со-крóй-ся: imperative of со-кры́ть-ся (or с-кры́ть-ся): imperfective со-крывáть-ся.

порá миновáлась: cf. xv 2 про-шлá порá: this imperfective is followed by two perfectives. One would expect минýлась here; but the past imperfective of this verb seems to be often used with the sense of the perfective.

11 ласкáя, pres. gerund.

древéсъ: дрéво, нéбо, and чýдо (a miracle) are three common neuter nouns which make their pl. in —есá, —éсъ.

12 съ, 'from.'

у-с-покóенныхъ: past part. pass. of у-с-покóить, 'to pacify.'

XVIII.

THE HAWK'S THOUGHTS.

The young man compares himself to a hawk in captivity, and asks whether he shall never have freedom to rove afar and see the world; he decides to spread his wings in defiance of all risks. There is a haunting quality in this little poem.

The metre is common in national songs: the line has two beats:

´ ◡ ‖ ´ ◡ ◡

1 бýду я жить, 'shall I continue to live?' The present of the perfective, i.e. про-живý, would give a different shade of meaning.

Note that бýду, like стáну, is always followed by the imperfective inf.: бýду про-жи́ть is not Russian at all.

2 си́днемъ, lit. 'as a sitter': instr. of си́день, which is applied to a bedridden person or a child that is long in walking.

дóма, 'at home,' adv.: домóй, 'homewards,' with a change of accent.

4 ни на чтó = дáромь, 'for nothing.' When никтó and ничтó are governed by a preposition, the prep. is inserted between ни- and the pronoun: hence ни за чтó, 'for nothing'; ни о чёмъ, 'about nothing' etc.

6 подъ окнóмъ: see n. to VIII 2.

7 по дорóгѣ, 'along the road': dat.

8 день: acc. of time.
9 у со́кола, 'belonging to the hawk.'
10 кры́лья, pl. of крыло́.
This stanza is quoted by Turgénev in Сме́рть (Запи́ски Охо́тника, p. 252).
11 путь, a very common masc. noun, is declined thus: путь, пути́, путём, пути́; pl. пути́, путе́й, путя́мъ etc.
12 за-ка́заны, 'forbidden': our *No Admittance* is тутъ ходи́ть за-ка́зано.
15 ма́чихой: the unkindness of a stepmother is proverbial in many languages: a Russian proverb says, мать гла́дитъ по ше́рсти, ма́чиха про́тивъ, 'a mother strokes the wool the right way, a stepmother the wrong way.'
18 хо́чет-ся = хочу́: the impers. verb is often used.
20 про́сит-ся: distinguish from проси́ть-ся (inf.). This word means 'to beg to go somewhere': in fairy stories, it is said of the ripe fruit, са́ми въ ротъ такъ и про́сятся, 'they positively beg to enter your mouth.'
21 она́: not, I think, a flesh-and-blood woman, but his own thought and desire personified.
24 льётъ (pronounce *lyot*), 3rd pers. sing., pres. ind. of лить.
рѣко́й, 'like a river': for this use of the instr., see n. to IV 12.
27 всё, 'continually': adv.
28 зовётъ: звать, 'to call,' makes зову́, зовёшь etc.
29 по́лно мнѣ сидѣ́ть, 'I have had enough of sitting': comp. XXII 19.
30 вѣкъ, 'for ever': adv.: it is a contraction of въ вѣкъ, 'during life.'
33 со двора́: see n. to XV 4.
по-йду́, 'I will go': the perfective of иду́, 'I go,' is formed by adding the prefix по-. He goes on foot; otherwise he would say по-ѣ́ду.
36 ужъ: not 'already,' but simply affirmative here: see n. to XIII 15.
вели́тъ, 'shall command': see n. to XI 3.

XIX.

POOR PEOPLE.

Alexander Shishkóv, the leader of a literary movement at the beginning of the 19th century, was appointed President of the Russian Academy in 1813, and, in that capacity, proposed Púshkin for membership in 1832.

I have taken his poem from a note by S. Aksákov to his *Years of Childhood*, p. 79. Aksákov's edition of the book which contained it was dated 1792. The poem is of interest, for its own merit; and it is also remarkable that it was written at least seven years before Púshkin was born, and is therefore many years earlier than any other of these poems.

4 хладъ = хóлодъ: see n. to IV 28.

с-носи́лъ, 'endured': so не-снóсный, 'unendurable': с-нести́ is the perfective form.

5 терпя́: pres. gerund of терпѣ́ть.

раз-ли́чны has dropped the termination -я, which it ought to have as an attributive adj.: see n. to III 12. There are other instances of this below.

7 мои́ must not be confused with мой, or both sense and metre will suffer.

8 что̀ покóй, 'what rest [is].'

9 всхóду: gen. in -у: the case is due to the negative verb: comp. XVI 16.

10 ни ра́зу, 'not once,' in the sense of 'never'; but не разъ, 'not once,' in the sense of 'more than once,' like Latin *non semel*.

ра́зу is gen. in -у.

про-спа́ть что-то is 'to miss a thing by sleeping,' as про-зѣва́ть, 'to miss a thing by carelessness,' lit. by yawning.

15 то..., то, 'at one time,...at another.'

дрóгнулъ, 'shivered,' a perfective of дрожа́ть: this verb, like many others, is formed by adding -ну-, the 'suffix of unity of action,' to the stem; and all such verbs are perfective, even without any prefix: comp. воз-дви́г-ну-лъ (l. 22). See Boyer, p. 23, n. 10.

16 весь, 'all over'; so всю in XII 2.

въ пыли́: the loc. after въ and на tends to accent the final syllable; so въ забытьи́, 'unconscious,' въ крови́, 'bleeding.'

17 за, 'engaged upon'; lit. 'at the back of.'

19, 20 He built strong dykes to prevent rivers from rushing wildly over their banks.

20 о-дѣлъ, perfective: о-дѣва́лъ, imperfective.
21 до́мы: дома́ is the commoner form of the plural. Stone houses in those days would belong only to rich people.
24 для свои́хъ, 'for my own family': see n. to v 44.
25 одна́ко is one of the words to which же (in the form жъ) is constantly tacked on: что is another.
э́то вре́мя: э́тотъ, generally meaning 'this,' is also used in many places where we should say 'that.'
26 бывъ, 'having been'; past gerund of быть: not, I think, in use now.
мо́лодъ, здоро́въ: the predicative forms (III 12) of молодо́й, здоро́вый.
27 бре́мя: one would expect бре́мени (gen.) after the negative verb; but the acc. is used also, though much more rarely, in this position.
28 сихъ: сей, сія́, сіё, is now expressed by э́тотъ, э́та, э́то: it is preserved in сей-ча́съ, 'immediately,' and in some stereotyped phrases, like сію́ мину́ту, 'this very minute.'
29 из-ли́шку: gen. in -у from из-ли́шекъ.
31 свою́, 'my': like свои́хъ (l. 24).
32 сытъ: the short, predicative, form of сы́тый.
33 мла́дость = мо́лодость: see n. to IV 28.
34 'It no longer exists.'
The unexpressed verb in this sentence is есть (is); and when the substantive verb 'to be' is negatived, the subject is in the gen., e.g. его́ тамъ не́ было, 'he was not there'; въ Россіи нѣтъ ничего́ подо́бнаго, 'there is nothing similar in Russia.' Thus ея́ (pronounce *ye-yó*), and not она́, must be used here. See n. to XXV 13.
бо́лѣе is stripped of its last syllable, for the sake of metre: the poets differ about this, some writing бо́лѣе and yet treating it as dissyllabic.
35 со-гну́ла, 'has bent': the perfective corresponds here to our perfect, in l. 33 to our aorist.
38 сиръ: predicative form of си́рый: the adj. is rare in prose, but the noun сирота́, 'orphan,' very common.
39 сме́рти: verbs of expecting take the gen.: comp. IX 10.
40 сталъ, 'has become.'
міръ, 'world,' is thus spelt, to distinguish it from миръ, 'peace': there is no other case in which і is used before a consonant.

XX.

THE BIRD'S VOICE.

The poet repeats Hood's lament:

'But now 'tis little joy
To know I'm further off from Heaven
Than when I was a boy.'

But he draws hope for the future from the song of the nightingale.

The metre is like that of xiv.

1 от-шумѣ́вшаго: gen. sing. masc., past part. active of от-шумѣ́ть, 'to cease to sound,' a perfective of шумѣ́ть. For the meaning of the prefix, cf. ступа́ть, 'to step,' от-ступа́ть, 'to step back,' 'to retreat.'

2 тихо́нько: dim. of ти́хо: Ти́хій Океа́нъ, 'the Pacific Ocean.'

текли́: this and the five following verbs are imperfectives, as they describe what was happening at a given time.

5 изъ-за, 'from behind': another compound prep. is изъ-подъ, 'from under'; изъ-подъ поду́шекъ, 'from under the pillows.'

6 какъ бу́дто: see n. to xii 9.

9 была́ ли душа́ моя́, 'whether my soul was...'; indirect questions are expressed very simply in Russian by ли which is placed second in the question; so чтобъ у-зна́ть, живъ ли я, 'in order to find out whether I was alive.'

тѣ го́ды, 'those past years': тотъ is the pronoun of the remote object, whether past or future: hence тотъ свѣтъ is 'the next world.'

11, 12 Both verbs in the conditional sentence are perfective: 'I would not have believed..., I would not have done'; вѣ́рить and дѣ́лать are the imperfectives.

12 мно́гаго, gen. of мно́гое, after the negative verb.

13 же, 'but.'

16 у-несло́, lit. 'it has carried away,' i.e. they have been carried away. Impersonal verbs are common in Russian, and the compounds of нести́ are very often so used: so мостъ с-несло́, 'the bridge was covered with snow'; дворъ за-несло́, 'the court was deep in snow.'

18 добрѣй (for добрѣе: see n. to xv 19), 'better,' 'kinder.' я былъ лу́чше would mean, 'I was handsomer'; but лу́чшій is the regular adjective meaning 'better.'

23 у-тѣ́шь-ся: imperative of у-тѣ́шить-ся.

сѣ́туй: imperative of сѣ́товать, which makes сѣ́тую, сѣ́туешь in indicative.

24 то вре́мя, 'that past time.'

вернёт-ся, 'will return': верну́ть-ся is perfective of вертѣ́ть-ся: for the suffix -ну-, see n. to XIX 15.

XXI.

WINTER EVENING.

Púshkin describes an evening such as he often spent in the winter of 1825, when he was living in a crazy old country-house belonging to his family, with no companion but his old nurse, Arína Ardaliónovna. She had told him fairy-tales and sung him songs in his infancy; and he tells us in *Eugene Onégin* (IV 35) that he read the poetry of his manhood to no one but his 'old nurse, the companion of his youth.' She died in 1829 and ought to be as famous in literary history as Molière's housekeeper.

The metre is trochaic:

´ ◡ | ´ ◡ | ´ ◡ | ´ ◡ |
´ ◡ | ´ ◡ | ´ ◡ | ´

1 кро́етъ: крыть, 'to cover,' makes кро́ю, кро́ешь etc.

2 крутя́: pres. gerund of крути́ть.

3 то́...то́: see XIX 15.

за-во́етъ and the three following verbs are all present-perfectives, so that each has a future sense; yet in English we should say, 'it howls,' 'it wails' etc.

This is a common idiom, however: see XXII 5. The perfective is used, because the actions described are not continuous: the wind howls for a moment, and then wails instead. But the sky remains covered with mist; therefore the imperfective кро́етъ is used in l. 1.

The imperfectives of the four verbs are выть, пла́кать, шумѣ́ть, стуча́ть.

6 соло́мой, 'with the straw.'

9–10 This house, which no longer exists, was called Mihailovskoe;

it was a wooden house of one storey and in bad repair in 1825. It was in the Government of Pskov.

12 прі-у-мо́лкла, 'have you been silent for a time': the last three words convey this meaning of the prefix при-: it has other meanings.

14 мой другъ: другъ, though masculine, is often addressed to a woman: по-дру́га is generally used of a woman's female friends. другъ implies special intimacy: not every прія́тель is by any means a другъ.

15 дре́млешь: 2nd pers. sing., pres. ind. of дрема́ть.

подъ, 'to the sound of': подъ more often takes acc. in this sense.

16 своего́, 'your': see n. to v 44.

17 вы́-пьемъ, 'let us drink': the 1st pers. pl. of the present-perfective expresses this meaning, either by itself or with the addition of -те: see XIII 13.

до́брая, 'kind,' the opposite of зла́я.

19 съ го́ря, 'from sorrow,' i.e. to drown sorrow.

21 с-пой, imperative of с-пѣть, which is perfective of пѣть, 'to sing': so с-ыгра́й намъ что́-нибудь, 'play us something,' с-ыгра́ть being perfective of игра́ть.

The two songs are traditional in Russia:

за́ моремъ сини́чка
не́ пышно жила́,

and

у́лицѣ по мостово́й
шла дѣви́ца за водо́й,

are the first lines of each.

22 за́ моремъ, 'across the sea': за robs мо́ремъ of its accent: so за́ городомъ, 'out of town.'

24 за водо́й, 'to fetch water': common use of за with instr.: so по-сла́ть за до́кторомъ, 'to send for a doctor.'

поу́тру here, but поутру́ in x 5.

шла, 'walked': past tense of идти́.

XXII.

THE POST-HOUSE.

Russian literature has many descriptions—Turgénev's *Karatáev* is one—of the intense boredom of travellers kept waiting at post-houses until they can get horses to proceed on their journey. The usual resource is the самова́ръ (tea-urn); but the writer does not mention even this.

Tolstói here uses another of Heine's ballad-metres, with a trochaic rhythm:

> Anfangs wollt' ich fast verzagen,
> Und ich glaubt', ich trüg es nie.
> –́ ⏑ | –́ ⏑ | –́ ⏑ | –́ ⏑ |
> –́ ⏑ | –́ ⏑ | –́ ⏑ | –́

1 что́ за: for this constr., see n. to IX 9.

2 како́й знако́мый, or какъ знако́мъ, but never какъ знако́мый: see n. to XI 6.

The traveller is painfully familiar with the aspect of such a room.

3 за стѣно́й, 'behind the wall,' i.e. in the next room.

4 ма́ятникъ: there is a clock on the wall, with a long pendulum which ticks.

5 сту́кнетъ: from сту́кнуть, a perfective of стуча́ть, formed with the suffix of single action, -ну-. 'It gives *one* tick to the right, *one* tick to the left,' will represent the difference between сту́кнетъ and стучи́тъ. See nn. to XIX 15 and XXI 3.

6 бу́дитъ: not to be confused with буди́ть (inf.).

7 въ нёмъ (pronounce *vnyom*), 'in it,' i.e. the ма́ятникъ.

8 за-твержённые: past part. pass. of за-тверди́ть.

10 до-горѣ́вшая, 'that has burnt down': the prefix до- is used constantly with this meaning of ending or completion: thus до-говори́ть, 'to end your speech.'

11 пёсъ (pronounce *pyoss*), gen. пса, is a more contemptuous name for a dog than соба́ка.

12 хо́дитъ, 'keeps moving': if it moved only once, идётъ would be used: see n. to VI 14.

стуча́: gerund of стуча́ть: сту́кнуть forms no pres. gerund.

14 всё, 'all the time'; adv.

17 гото́вы, '[are] ready.'

18 сѣлъ, 'I have taken my seat': past tense of сѣсть, the perfective of сади́ть-ся.

киби́тка, a carriage; it is also the name for a Tatar hut.

скачу́: from скака́ть.

19 по́лно = 'too bad!'

такъ ли, 'can it be true?'

22 круго́мъ: instr. used as an adverb.

XXIII.

A MIDNIGHT THOUGHT.

Another picture of an interior by the same writer. In a sleeping house, in stormy weather, the owner looks out into the dark and thinks—thinks of his own death and of the fate which will then befall his old house.

The metre is that of XIII, XIV, and XX.

1 на дворѣ́: see n. to XV 4.

2 спятъ, 'the people are asleep': an indefinite plural for subject: cf. III 3.

3 вз-дохну́въ: past gerund of вз-дохну́ть: the pres. gerund, вз-дыха́я, is formed, as usual, from the imperfective.

под-хожу́: compounds of ходи́ть are imperfective, compounds of идти́ perfective.

4 ви́денъ, predicative form of ви́дный.

6 The verb 'to be' being here negatived, the subject (звѣ́здочки) is in the gen: see nn. to XIX 34, XXV 13.

9 бить, 'to beat,' makes бью, бьёшь, бьётъ; so пить makes пью, пьёшь, пьётъ.

11 за шка́помъ, 'behind the cupboard.'

12 бума́жный means (1) made of paper; (2) made of cotton: the latter is probably meant here: Púshkin, describing an old-fashioned house, speaks of што́фные обо́и (*Onégin*, II 2).

13 онѣ́, 'they,' the mice, мышь being fem.

14 у-мрётъ, 'shall die': Russian, like Latin, uses the future where we prefer the present: у-мру́, 'I will die,' and у-мира́ю, 'I am dying,' show the two aspects of this verb.

15 по-ки́нетъ, 'will desert'; but по-кида́етъ, 'is deserting.'

16 жилъ, 'used to live': imperfective.

родъ: the rhyme shows here (and in l. 4) that -дъ is sounded like our *t*.

17, 18 Both verbs are future in sense, belonging to the perfectives, за-пустѣ́ть and за-гло́хнуть: in the latter, the inf. differs from 3rd pers. pl. of the pres. ind. by the last letter only.

18 ступе́нь must be distinguished from сте́пень: both are fem. and declined alike, and akin in meaning; they differ in their first vowel and in accent.

XXIV.

THE EXILE.

This is the poem which was selected for special praise by Turgénev, when he published a criticism of Tyúchev's poetry in 1854. He then set Tyúchev at the head of living Russian poets, above Nekrásov, Maíkov, and Fet. 'We do not prophesy popularity for Tyúchev,' he wrote; 'but we do prophesy the deep and warm sympathy of all to whom Russian poetry is dear; and such poems as *The Exile*, and others, will go through Russia from end to end, and will survive much contemporary literature which now seems permanent and enjoys resounding success.'

1 по-шли́ Господь, 'may God send': по-шли́ is imperative of по-сла́ть, and the 2nd pers. is used where most languages use the 3rd: comp. the common phrase не дай Богъ, 'God forbid,' дай being 2nd pers. of the imperative.

For the voc. Го́споди, see n. to XII 15.

2 тому́, кто: the regular relative pronoun is кото́рый, —ая, —ое; but кто, the interrogative pr., is used as a relative after certain antecedents, of which тотъ is the commonest. Note that the antecedent to кто may be of any number or gender.

3 са́ду: gen. with -у ending, distinguished by accent from the loc. in -у́ (въ саду́, 'in the garden'), but identical with the dat. of садъ.

10 сѣ́нью, 'with shade': instr. of сѣнь, a rare word in prose.

раз-росли́сь: the prefix denotes the expansion and spreading growth of the trees.

12 по-ви́съ, lit. 'has been hung,' i.e. hovers: по-ви́с-ну-ть, perfective of висѣ́ть, makes, in its past tense, по-ви́съ, по-ви́сла, по-ви́сло.

14 мани́тъ: the accent ма́нитъ is often preferred.

15 пыль, 'dust,' is often used of particles of spray or fine snow.

16 главы́, the older form of головы́: see n. to IV 28: the gen. is due to the negative verb.

не о-свѣжитъ, 'will not refresh': the verb is perfective.

XXV.

THE TRIUMPH OF LOVE.

Semyón Nádson (1862–1887) enjoyed during his short life greater contemporary reputation than has ever been gained by any Russian poet. But life brought him little happiness. He suffered from consumption for six years before his death, living at health-resorts and undergoing repeated operations. We are told that his fame did not avail to lighten the thought of coming death.

This famous poem is considered Nádson's masterpiece. It is nobly conceived, and moves to a most noble music.

The metre is made up of pure anapaests:

⏑ ⏑ ⏑́ | ⏑ ⏑ ⏑́ | ⏑ ⏑ ⏑́ | ⏑ ⏑ ⏑́ |
⏑ ⏑ ⏑́ | ⏑ ⏑ ⏑́ | ⏑ ⏑ ⏑́

1 страда́ющій: pres. participle of страда́ть.

2 кто бъ ты ни́ былъ, 'whoever thou art': comp. III 10, VIII 9, and see n. to the latter passage.

не па́дай: imperfective, as usual, in the prohibition: see n. to III 30.

душо́й, 'in heart': ду́хомъ is used in prose: онъ упа́лъ ду́хомъ, 'he lost heart.'

3 пусть...: 'let falsehood and evil reign': cf. III 31.

The 3rd pers., sing. and pl., of the imperative is expressed by пусть or пуска́й (imperatives of пусти́ть and пускать) followed by a 3rd pers. of pres. ind.; e.g. пусть на-пи́шетъ, 'let him write.' The following verb is generally perfective, as in III 31; but this is not always so: here both царя́тъ and струи́тся are imperfectives; and such instances are not rare.

5 The verb есть is suppressed as usual, and the participles have their predicative form, instead of раз-би́тый and по-ру́ганный. For the form of sentence, cf.

пуска́й холо́дною землёю
за-сы́панъ я,

'let me be covered over with cold earth' (Lérmontov).

7 вѣ́рь: imperative of вѣ́рить.

на-ста́нетъ, 'will come': from на-ста́ть (perfective).

пора́, 'the right time,' 'the hour.'

по-ги́бнетъ, 'will be destroyed': from по-ги́бнуть (perfective).

Баа́лъ = the Powers of Evil.

8 вернёт-ся: see xx 24.

9 въ = 'wearing,' as often.

цѣпе́й, gen. pl.

11 міръ: see n. to xix 40.

12 съ = 'holding.'

13 не бу́детъ puts all the nouns which form its complement in the gen.: see n. to xix 34: слёзъ не́ было, 'there were no tears'; нѣтъ слёзъ, 'there are no tears'; не бу́детъ слёзъ, 'there will be no tears.'

14 'Crossless graves,' i.e. nameless graves, are those of suicides: cf. Lérmontov,

> крова́вая меня́ моги́ла ждётъ,
> моги́ла безъ моли́твъ и безъ креста́

(a bloody grave awaits me, a grave without prayers and without a cross).

моги́лъ: gen. pl. with zero ending.

15 мертвя́щей, 'killing': gen. sing. fem., pres. part. act., of мертви́ть.

16 позо́рный столбъ, 'a pillory.'

17 мечто́й might have been written here equally well: 'the predicate in Russian is put in the nominative or the instrumental, and often the choice between the two cases is immaterial,' Boyer, p. 11.

18 одна́ = 'merely.'

19 о-гляни́-сь, 'look all round': imperative of о-гляну́ть-ся, perfective.

ужъ, 'by this time.'

гнетётъ: 3rd pers. sing., pres. ind., of гнести́.

21 у-ста́нетъ, 'will grow weary,' from у-ста́ть: so у-ви́димъ, кто изъ насъ у-ста́нетъ пре́жде, 'we shall see which of us will tire first': this and the next three verbs are all perfective presents: they contain a prophecy and refer to the future.

23 под-ня́ть (perfective) makes под-ниму́, под-ни́мешь, под-ни́метъ; 'he is raising' is под-нима́етъ, imperfective.

24 мольбо́й: по́лный, 'full,' may take either the instr., as here, or the gen.

APPENDIX I.

ASPECTS—IMPERFECTIVE AND PERFECTIVE.

1. Every verbal notion may be expressed in Russian in either of two Aspects, the Imperfective and Perfective; and every Russian verb belongs to one or other of these two Aspects.

2. Most perfective verbs are compound, being formed by the addition of a prefix (such as на-, по-, воз-, вы-, and others) to a simple and imperfective verb: thus писа́ть (*to write*) is imperfective, but на-писа́ть (*to write*) is perfective[1].

3. A verb in the imperfective aspect expresses continued action:

я писа́лъ весь день,
I was writing all day.

A verb in the perfective aspect expresses completed action:

вчера́ я на-писа́лъ къ вамъ,
I wrote to you yesterday.

4. The present tense of every imperfective is present in meaning: e.g.

я пишу́,
I write, or, *I am writing.*

But the present tense of every perfective is future in meaning:

я на-пишу́,
I shall write.

5. The prefix which serves to convert an imperfective verb into a perfective loses its special meaning.

Thus на-, when used as a prefix, generally bears the meaning of *on* or *against*; but я на-пишу́ means simply, *I shall write.*

6. Any other prefix than на-, placed before -писа́ть, retains its meaning: hence о-писа́ть = *to describe*, пере-писа́ть = *to copy*, под-писа́ть = *to sign*, etc.

7. Those prefixes which retain their meaning also change the imperfective verb, e.g. писа́ть, to a perfective.

Hence я о-пишу́ means *I shall describe.*

8. How then is it possible to express *I am describing*?

This is done by a change in the stem of the verb[2].

Either -ив- or -ыв is inserted between the stem and

[1] писа́ть=*γράφειν*, and на-писа́ть=*γράψαι*: the perfective is in fact an 'aorist voice.'

[2] Comp. the change by which *βάλλειν*, when compounded with any other element than a preposition, becomes -*βολεῖν*.

termination of the simple verb; and every compound of this form is imperfective, and the prefixes keep their meaning: e.g.

о-пи́с-ыв-аю, *I describe*,
пере-пи́с-ыв-аю, *I copy*,
под-пи́с-ыв-аю, *I sign*.

9. It has been explained already that the perfective has no true present. Similarly, the imperfective has no true future, but makes one with an auxiliary verb, as English does:

бу́ду писа́ть, *I shall write* (not once, but from time to time).

N.B. Auxiliary verbs, such as бу́ду, ста́ну, пере-ста́ну, etc., are never followed by a perfective infinitive.

10. Both aspects form an imperative:

(i) пиши́, пиши́те;
(ii) на-пиши́, на-пиши́те.

Of these, the perfective imperative, на-пиши́, is the more peremptory.

11. Both aspects form a past tense:

(i) я писа́лъ, *I was writing, I used to write, I tried to write.*

N.B. This aspect is commonly used in negative and interrogative sentences, even where the sense of 'continuance' is not obvious.

(ii) я на-писа́лъ, *I wrote, I have written, I had written.*

12. Both aspects form past participles, active and passive, and a past gerund:

(i) писа́вшій, пи́санный, писа́въ,
(ii) на-писа́вшій, на-пи́санный, на-писа́въ.

13. But the pres. participles and pres. gerund,

пи́шущій, писа́емый and пиша́,

are formed only from the imperfective aspect.

14. In every part of the verb which is found in both aspects, completed action is expressed by the perfective, and continuous action by the imperfective. The distinction is generally clear enough; but, in the case of the past tense and the infinitive, it is difficult at times to account for the aspect chosen.

Note. Much fuller information will be found in Forbes' *Russian Grammar*, §§ 101–117; see also Boyer's *Russian Reader*, the Index under the heading *Aspect.*

APPENDIX II.

The two following translations by Mr Maurice Baring are reprinted, by permission, from his *Outline of Russian Literature* (Messrs Williams and Norgate), pp. 120 and 236.

III.

I want to be alone with you,
  A moment quite alone.
The minutes left to me are few,
  They say I'll soon be gone.
And you'll be going home on leave,
Then say...but why? I do believe
There's not a soul who'll greatly care
To hear about me over there.

And yet, if someone asks you there,
  Let us suppose they do—
Tell them a bullet hit me here,
  The chest,—and it went through.
And say I died and for the Tsar,
And say what fools the doctors are;—
And that I shook you by the hand,
And thought about my native land.

My father and my mother, too!
  They may be dead by now;
To tell the truth, it wouldn't do
  To grieve them anyhow.
If one of them is living, say
I'm bad at writing home, and they
Have sent us to the front, you see,—
And that they needn't wait for me.

We had a neighbour, as you know,
  And you remember I
And she...How very long ago
  It is we said goodbye!
She won't ask after me, nor care,
But tell her ev'rything, don't spare
Her empty heart; and let her cry;—
To her it doesn't signify.

XIV.

Through the slush and the ruts of the highway,
  By the side of the dam of the stream,
Where the fisherman's nets are drying,
  The carriage jogs on, and I dream.

I dream, and I look at the highway,
  At the sky that is sullen and grey,
At the lake with its shelving reaches,
  And the curling smoke far away.

By the dam, with a cheerless visage,
  Walks a Jew, who is ragged and sere.
With a thunder of foam and of splashing,
  The waters race over the weir.

A boy over there is whistling
  On a hemlock flute of his make;
And the wild ducks get up in a panic
  And call as they sweep from the lake.

And near the old mill some workmen
  Are sitting upon the green ground,
With a wagon of sacks, a cart horse
  Plods past with a lazy sound.

It all seems to me so familiar,
  Although I have never been here,
The roof of that house out yonder,
  And the boy, and the wood, and the weir.

And the voice of the grumbling mill-wheel,
  And that rickety barn, I know,
I have been here and seen this already,
  And forgotten it all long ago.

The very same horse here was dragging
  Those sacks with the very same sound,
And those very same workmen were sitting
  By the rickety mill on the ground.

And that Jew, with his beard, walked past me,
  And those waters raced through the weir;
Yes, all this has happened already,
  But I cannot tell when or where.

VOCABULARY

Most of the abbreviations will be readily understood: *instr.* stands for the instrumental case, and *loc.* for the locative or prepositional.

The gender of nouns is given only where the termination of the nominative leaves the gender doubtful.

Where two infinitive forms of the verb are given together, the first is always imperfective, the second, in brackets, perfective.

The order of the alphabet is: а, б, в, г, д, е, ж, з, и, і, й, к, л, м, н, о, п, р, с, т, у, ф, х, ц, ч, ш, щ, ъ, ы, ь, ѣ, э, ю, я. Of these, й, ъ, ы, ь, are never initial.

а, *but*, *and*.
ака́ція, *acacia*.
а́лчный, *thirsty*.
а́нгелъ, *angel*.
анча́ръ, *the poison-tree*.
Арзру́мъ, *Erzerum*.

Баа́лъ, *Baal*.
база́ръ, —а, *market-place*.
бараба́нить, *to drum*.
ба́юшки-баю́, *hush-a-by*.
без-завѣ́тный, *infinite*.
без-коне́чно, *infinitely*.
без-кре́стный, *without a cross*.
без-про-свѣ́тный, *uncivilised*, *hopeless*.
без-у́мный, *senseless*.
без-утѣ́шно, *inconsolably*.
безъ, prep. with gen., *without*.
бе́регъ (or брегъ), pl. берега́, *bank*.
берёза, *birch tree*.
беру́: pres. indic. of брать.
бесѣ́довать (по-бесѣ́довать), *to converse*.
би́тва, *battle*.
бить (по-би́ть), *to beat*.
благо-во́нный, *fragrant*.
благо-словя́ть (благослови́ть), *to bless*.
бле́щутъ: see блиста́ть.
близъ, prep. with gen., *near*.
блиста́ть, блиста́ю and блещу́, бле́щешь, *to shine*.
блужда́ть (по-блужда́ть), *to wander*.

блѣ́дный, *pale.*
бога́тство, *wealth.*
богаты́рь, —я́, m., *hero.*
Богъ, *God.*
боево́й, —а́я, —о́е, *of battle.*
бой, бо́я, *battle.*
бо́лѣ (and бо́лѣе), adv., *more.*
борода́тый, *bearded.*
боро́ться (по-боро́ться), *to wrestle.*
боръ, *pine-forest.*
борьба́, *a struggle.*
боязли́во, *timidly.*
боя́ться (по-боя́ться), *to fear.*
бра́нный, *warlike.*
бра́тецъ, —ца, *little brother, comrade.*
братъ, *brother, comrade.*
брать (взять), *to take.*
бредётъ: from брести́.
бре́мя, —ени, n., *burden.*
брести́ (по-брести́), *to drag oneself along.*
бри́тый, *shaven.*
бровь, —и, f., *eyebrow.*
буди́ть (раз-буди́ть), бужу́, бу́дишь, *to arouse.*
будь: imperative of быть.
бума́жный, *of paper, of stuff.*
бу́ря, *storm.*
бы or бъ: conditional particle.
былъ, была́, бы́ло: past tense of быть.
быть, *to be*: fut. бу́ду, —ешь; imperative будь.
быть мо́жетъ, *may-be, perhaps.*
бью, бьёшь, бьётъ: from бить.
бѣгъ, *course.*
бѣда́, *calamity.*
бѣ́дный, *poor.*
бѣжа́ть (по-бѣжа́ть), *to run.*
бѣ́лый, *white.*
бѣлѣ́ть, *to be white.*
бѣси́ться (вз-бѣси́ться), *to be furious.*

валъ, —а, *a wave.*
ввечеру́, adv., *at evening.*
в-води́ть, *to introduce.*
в-дали́, adv., *in the distance.*
в-даль, adv., *far.*
в-доль, prep. with gen., *along.*
вдругъ, *suddenly.*
в-дѣва́ть (в-дѣть), *to push in.*
везти́ (по-везти), *to draw along.*
велѣ́ть, *to command.*
веретено́, *spindle.*
вертѣ́ть (верну́ть), *to turn*; верну́ться, *to return.*
ве́село, adv., *merrily.*
весе́нній, —яя, —ее, *of spring.*
весна́, *spring.*
весь, вся, всё, *all.*
ве́тхiй, *ancient.*
вече́рній, *of evening.*
вз-бѣси́ться: see бѣси́ться.
вз-глядъ, *a look.*
вз-дыха́ть (вз-дохну́ть), *to sigh.*

вз-летѣ́ть, *to take flight.*
вз-мета́ть (вз-метну́ть), *to stir up.*
взоръ, *look, glance.*
ви́дно, *clearly.*
ви́дный, *visible.*
видъ, *aspect, sight.*
ви́дѣть (у-ви́дѣть), *to see.*
вино́, *wine, spirits.*
висѣ́ть (по-ви́снуть), *to hang* (intr.).
ви́хорь, —хря, m., *whirlwind.*
влады́ка, m., *lord.*
вла́стный, *powerful, authoritative.*
в-лѣ́во, adv., *to the left.*
внима́тельный, *attentive.*
вода́, *water.*
воз-враща́ться (воз-врати́ться), *to return.*
воз-двига́ть (воз-дви́гнуть), *to erect.*
во́з-духъ, *air.*
возду́шный, *airy, unsubstantial.*
возьму́, возьмёшь, pres. ind. of взять: see брать.
во́инъ, *warrior.*
во-кру́гъ, adv., *around.*
Во́лга, *the Volga.*
волнова́ться (вз-волнова́ться), *to be excited.*
волше́бница, *sorceress.*
во́ля, *freedom.*
вонъ, adv., *out.*
ворча́ть (ворчи́ть), *to scold*
Восто́къ, —о́ка, *the East.*
вотъ, *lo! see!*
в-перёдъ, adv., *forward.*
в-пра́во, adv., *to the right.*
врагъ, —а́, *enemy.*
вражда́, *enmity.*
вре́мя, вре́мени, n., *time.*
в-руча́ть (в-ручи́ть), *to hand over.*
всё, adv., *constantly.*
всё, adj.: neut. of весь.
вселе́нная, *the universe.*
в-скользь, adv., *in passing.*
вс-по́мнишь: see по́мнить.
в-стрѣча́ть (в-стрѣ́тить), *to meet.*
вс-ходи́ть (взо-йти́), *to rise up.*
вс-ходъ, —а, *rising.*
всѣ: pl. of весь.
всю: fem. acc. of весь.
вся́кій, *every, any.*
въ (and во), prep. with loc. or acc., *in, into, to, on.*
въ пол-го́лоса, *in a low voice.*
вы́-летъ, *flight*; на вы́-летъ, *right through.*
вы́-пьемъ: see пить.
высо́кій, *tall, high.*
высота́, *height.*
вы-сыла́ть (вы́-слать), *to send out.*
выть (за-вы́ть), *to howl.*
вы-ходи́ть (вы́-йдти), *to go out, come out.*

вѣ́дьма, *witch.*

вѣ́жда, *eyelid.*

вѣ́къ, adv., *all through life.*

вѣне́цъ, —ца́, *crown.*

вѣ́ра, *faith.*

вѣ́рить (по-вѣ́рить), *to believe.*

вѣтвь, —и, f., *branch.*

вѣтеро́къ, —ка́, *breeze.*

вѣ́теръ, —тра, *wind, breeze.*

вѣ́чно, adv., *for ever.*

гада́ть (по-гада́ть), *to tell fortunes.*

гаре́мъ, —а, *harem.*

гдѣ́, *where.*

гдѣ́-то, *somewhere.*

ги́бель, —и, f., *destruction.*

ги́бнуть (по-ги́бнуть), *to be destroyed.*

глава́ = голова́.

глазо́къ, —ка́, *little eye.*

глазъ, —а, *eye*: pl. глаза́.

гласи́ть, *to speak.*

гло́хнуть (за-гло́хнуть), *to grow deaf.*

глядѣ́ть (по-глядѣ́ть), *to look.*

гна́ть (по-гна́ть), *to chase.*

гнести́ (у-гнести́), *to oppress.*

гнётъ, —а, *oppression.*

гнѣвъ, *wrath.*

говори́ть (сказа́ть), *to say, to speak.*

го́воръ, *clack.*

годъ, —а, *year.*

голова́, *head.*

го́лосъ, *voice*: pl. голоса́.

голубо́й, —а́я, —о́е, *blue.*

гоне́цъ, гонца́, *courier, herald.*

гоню́, го́нишь: pres. indic. of гнать.

го́рдый, *proud.*

го́ре, —я, *grief.*

го́рькій, *bitter.*

горѣ́ть (с-горѣ́ть), *to burn* (intr.).

горю́чій, *burning.*

Госпо́дь, Го́спода, voc. Го́споди, *the Lord, God.*

госте-пріи́мный, *hospitable.*

гото́виться (при-гото́виться), *to get ready.*

гото́вый, *ready.*

гре́бля, *a weir.*

грёза, *a dream.*

гре́зиться, *to dream.*

гро́зный, *threatening.*

громъ, *thunder-clap.*

гротъ, *grotto.*

грудь, —и, f., *breast.*

гру́стный, *sad.*

губа́, *lip.*

губи́ть (по-губи́ть), *to destroy, ruin.*

гумно́, *threshing-floor.*

густо́й, —а́я, —о́е, *thick.*

гяу́ръ, *Giaour.*

да, *yes*; *but, and.*

дава́ть (да́ть), *to give.*

давнó, adv., *long ago.*
далёкій, *distant.*
дáльній, *distant.*
дамъ, *I will give*: see давáть.
данъ, —á, —ó, *given.*
дáромъ, adv., *in vain, for no reason.*
два, двѣ, два, *two.*
движéнье, *movement.*
дворъ, *court-yard*: на дворѣ́, *out of doors*; со дворá, *off the place.*
день, дня, m., *day*: pl. дни, дней, днямъ.
дерéвня, *village.*
дéрево, —а, n., *tree*: pl. дерéвья.
джигúтъ, *cavalier.*
дúвный, *wondrous.*
дúкій, *wild, savage.*
дитя́, —тя́ти, n., *child*: plur. дѣ́ти.
длúнный, *long.*
для, prep. with gen., *for the sake of, for.*
дневнóй, —áя, —óе, *of day.*
дней: see день.
до, prep. with gen., *until.*
дóблестный, *valiant.*
дóбрый, *good, kind.*
довóльно, adv., *it is enough.*
довóльный, *sufficient.*
до-горѣ́ть, *to burn low.*
дождь, —я́, m., *rain.*
дóлго, adv., *for long.*
долго-терпѣ́ніе, *long-suffering, endurance.*
долúна, *a dell.*
дóма, adv., *at home.*
домóй, adv., *home, to one's house.*
домъ, —а, *house.*
дорóга, *road, journey.*
дорóжка, *path.*
дорóжный, *of the road, travelling.*
дрéвній, —няя, —нее, *ancient.*
дрéво, *tree*: pl. древесá, —вéсъ.
дремáть (за-дремáть), *to sleep.*
дремлú, imperative of дремáть.
дремучій, *thick, close.*
дрóгнуть, *to shiver*
дрожáть (по-дрожáть), *to shiver.*
другóй, —áя, —óе, *other, second.*
другъ, —а, *friend.*
дýдка, *a pipe.*
дýма, *a thought.*
дýмать (по-дýмать), *to think.*
духъ, —а, *scent.*
душá, *soul, darling.*
душúстый, *fragrant.*
ды́мной, *smoke-like.*
дымóкъ, —кá, *faint smoke.*
дымъ, —а, *smoke.*

дыша́ть (по-дыша́ть), *to breathe.*

дѣви́ца, *girl.*

дѣлать (с-дѣлать), *to do.*

дѣтскій, *childlike.*

евну́хъ, *eunuch.*

его́, *him, it*: acc. of онъ.

его́ (gen.), *of him, his.*

едва́, adv., *hardly.*

её: acc. of она́.

ей: dat. of она́.

ему́: dat. of онъ.

е́сли, *if.*

есть, *there is.*

ещё, *still*; ещё не, *not yet.*

ея́: gen. of она́.

жа́воронокъ, —ка, *lark.*

жа́ждущій, *thirsty.*

жаль, adv., = *I regret.*

жалѣть (по-жалѣть), *to pity.*

жа́ркій, *burning.*

жа́рче, *more hotly*: comp. of жа́рко.

жаръ, *heat.*

жда́ть (подо-жда́ть), *to expect, await.*

же (and жъ), enclitic particle, *and, but.*

жена́, *wife*: pl. жёны.

жечь (с-жечь), *to burn*: pres. ind. жгу, жжёшь.

живо́й, —ая, —о́е, *living.*

жидъ, —а́, *a Jew.*

жи́зненный, *of life.*

жизнь, —ни, f., *life.*

жить (про-жи́ть), *to live*: живу́, живёшь.

житьё, —ья́, *way of life.*

жужжа́нье, *humming.*

жъ = же.

за, prep. with acc. and instr., *behind, beyond, for.*

забве́нье, *oblivion.*

за-бира́ться (за-бра́ться), *to clamber up.*

забо́та, *care.*

за-быва́ть (за-бы́ть), *to forget.*

за-бы́тый, *forgotten.*

за-бы́тье, *oblivion*: въ забытьи́, *unconscious.*

за-вито́къ, —ка́, *a curl.*

за-во́етъ: see выть.

за́втра, *to-morrow.*

за-выва́нье, *howling.*

за-вѣшенный, *curtained.*

за-вѣща́ніе, *a last will.*

за-гло́хнуть, *to be choked.*

за-ду́мчиво, *thoughtfully.*

за-ка́заный, *forbidden.*

за-ка́ливать (за-кали́ть), *to temper (of steel).*

за-крыва́ть (за-кры́ть), *to close.*

за-лива́ться (за-ли́ться), *to sing lustily.*

за-мира́ть (за-мере́ть), *to die away.*

за-мѣча́ть (за-мѣ́тить), *to notice.*

За́падъ, *the West.*

за-пла́четъ: from за-пла́кать: see пла́кать.

за-позда́лый, *belated.*

за-пустѣва́ть (за-пустѣ́ть), *to become empty.*

за-сну́ть: see за-сыпа́ть.

за-ставать (за-ста́ть), *to find, come upon.*

за-стуча́ть: see стуча́ть.

за-стыва́ть (за-сты́ть), *to coagulate.*

за-суети́ться, *to become busy.*

за-сыпа́ть (за-сну́ть), *to go to sleep.*

за-тве́рживать (за-тверди́ть), *to learn by heart.*

за-тиха́ть (за-ти́хнуть), *to quiet down.*

за-тя́гивать (за-тяну́ть), *to strike up.*

за-хва́тывать (за-хвати́ть), *to catch up.*

за-хлеба́ться (за-хлебну́ться), *to be choked.*

за-чѣ́мъ, *why?*

за-шуми́тъ: see шумѣ́ть.

зва́ть (по-зва́ть), *to summon.*

зво́нкій, *loud, ringing.*

звукъ, —а, *sound.*

звуча́ть (про-звуча́ть), *to sound.*

звѣзда́, *star.*

звѣ́здочка, *little star.*

звѣ́рь, —я, m., *wild beast*

здоро́вый, *healthy.*

здѣ́сь, *here.*

зелёный, *green.*

зе́лень, —и, f., *verdure.*

зеленѣ́ть, *to grow green.*

земля́, —и́, *land, earth.*

зима́, *winter.*

зи́мній, *of winter.*

злакъ, *grass.*

зли́ться (об-о-зли́ться), *to be angry.*

зло, —а, *evil.*

злой, —а́я, —о́е, *wicked, cruel.*

змій, —ія, *serpent.*

знако́мый, *familiar.*

знать, *to know.*

зна́чить, *to signify.*

зной, зно́я, *sultry heat.*

зно́йный, *sultry.*

зовётъ: pres. ind. of звать.

золоти́стый, *golden.*

золоти́ть (по-золоти́ть), *to gild.*

золото́й, —а́я, —о́е, *golden.*

зо́рька, *dear one.*

зрѣ́ть, *to behold.*

и, *and, even, also.*

игра́ть (с-ыгра́ть), *to play.*

идеалъ, *ideal.*

идти́ (по-йти́), иду́, идёшь, *to come, go (on foot).*

из-гнанникъ, *an exile.*

из-дава́ть (из-да́ть), *to give forth.*

из-ли́шекъ, —шка, *excess.*

изм-ѣ́на, *treason.*

из-мѣня́ть (из-мѣни́ть), *to betray.*

из-о́-рванный, *ragged.*

изъ, prep. with gen., *from, from among.*

изъ-за, prep. with gen., *from behind.*

и́ли (and иль), *or.*

и́ми: instr. plur. of онъ.

имъ: instr. sing. and dat. pl. of онъ.

имѣ́ть, *to possess.*

ино-племе́нный, *foreign.*

иска́ть (по-иска́ть), *to seek.*

ис-пу́гъ, —a, *terror.*

ис-ходи́ть, *to traverse on foot.*

ихъ: gen. and acc. pl. of онъ, она́.

ихъ, *of them, their.*

Кавка́зъ, *the Caucasus.*

каза́къ, —á, *Cossack.*

каза́ться, *to seem*; ка́жется, *it seems.*

каза́чій, —а́чья, —а́чье, adj., *Cossack.*

какой, —а́я, —о́е, *what, which.*

какъ, *how, when, as.*

какъ бу́дто, *as if.*

какъ бы, *as if.*

ка́менный, *of stone.*

ка́мень, —мня, m., *stone.*

ка́пать (за-ка́пать), *to drip*: pres. ind. ка́паю, —паешь, and ка́плю, —плешь.

ка́пля, —и, *a drop.*

карти́на, *a picture.*

киби́тка, *travelling carriage.*

кинжа́лъ, *dagger.*

класть (по-ложи́ть), *to lay, place.*

клёнъ, —a, *a maple.*

клочо́къ, —ка́, *fragment.*

кля́ча, *a sorry horse.*

ко́ваный, *mailed.*

кова́рный, *deceitful.*

кова́рство, *cunning.*

ковы́ль, —я́, m., *prairie grass.*

когда́, *when*; когда́-то, *long ago.*

коло́дникъ, *a convict.*

колыбе́ль, f., *cradle.*

колѣ́но, *knee*: pl. колѣ́ни.

коля́ска, *open carriage.*

конво́йный, *a guard.*

коне́цъ, конца́, *end.*

кончи́на, *death.*

кора́, *bark.*

ко́рень, —рня, m., pl. ко́рни, *root.*

корми́ть (на-корми́ть), *to feed, support.*

край, кра́я, *country.*

красота́, *beauty.*

кре́стный, *of the Cross.*

крестъ, —á, *cross.*
крикъ, —а, *cry.*
кричáть (за-кричáть), *to shout.*
крóвля, *roof.*
кровь, —и, f., *blood.*
крóетъ: pres. ind. of крыть.
кругóмъ, adv., *entirely, around.*
крýжка, *drinking cup.*
крути́ть (за-крути́ть), *to whirl about.*
крылó, *wing*: pl. кры́лья.
крыльцó, *balcony.*
крыть (по-кры́ть), *to cover.*
кры́ша, *roof.*
кто, *who, any.*
ктó-нибудь, *someone.*
кудá, *whither.*
кукýшка, *cuckoo.*
кустъ, —á, *bush.*
къ (ко), prep. with dat., *to, towards.*

лазýрный, *blue.*
лазýрь, —и, f., *blue sky.*
ласкáть (по-ласкáть), *to caress.*
лачýжка, *tumble-down house.*
лáять (за-лáять), *to bark.*
легкó, *easily, lightly.*
лёгъ, леглá, леглó, past tense of лечь: see ложи́ться.
лежáть (по-лежáть), *to lie.*
лéкарь, —я, *doctor.*
лéпетъ, *babble.*
летѣ́ть (по-летѣ́ть), *to fly*: pres. ind. лечý, лети́шь.
ли (and —ль), interrogative particle.
ликýющій, *triumphant.*
ликъ, *face.*
листóчекъ, —чка, *leaf.*
листъ, —á, *leaf, foliage*: pl. ли́стья, —евъ.
ли́стье, —я, *foliage.*
лить (про-ли́ть), *to pour.*
ли́ться (по-ли́ться), *to flow.*
лихóй, —áя, —óе, *cruel.*
лицó, *face.*
лишь, *only.*
лобъ, лба, *forehead.*
ложи́ться (лечь), *to lie down.*
лóно, *breast.*
лошáдка, *horse.*
лóшадь, —и, f., *horse.*
лугови́на, *a stretch of grass.*
лукáвый, *cunning.*
лунá, *moon.*
лучъ, —á, *ray.*
лы́ко, n. plur. лы́ки, *matting.*
ль = ли.
лью́тся: 3rd plur., pres. ind. of ли́ться.
лѣни́вый, *idle.*
лѣсъ, —а, *a wood.*
лѣ́тніи, —яя, —ее, *of summer.*
лѣ́то, *summer*: pl. лѣтá, *years.*
люби́ть (по-люби́ть), *to love.*
любóвь, любви́, f., *love.*
лю́ди, —éй, *people*: pl. of человѣ́къ.

люстра, *chandelier.*
лютый, *cruel.*

Майскій, adj., *of May.*
малый, *little.*
мальчикъ, *boy.*
малютка, *little one.*
манить (по-манить), *to beckon to.*
мать, матери, *mother.*
махать (махнуть), *to wave.*
мачиха, *step-mother.*
маятникъ, *pendulum.*
мгла, —ы, *mist, darkness.*
медленно, adv., *slowly.*
между (and межъ), prep. with instr., *between.*
мельница, *a mill.*
меня: gen. and acc. of я.
меркнуть, *to grow dark.*
мёртвый, *dead.*
мертвящій, *killing.*
мести (вы-мести), *to sweep.*
мечта, *a dream.*
мечъ, —а, *a sword.*
милый, *dear.*
мимо, prep. with gen., *past.*
миновать (минуть), *to pass away.*
міръ, *the world.*
младенецъ, —нца, *infant.*
младость = молодость.
много-дорожный, *of many ways.*
многое, n. adj., *much.*
мной (and мною): instr. of я.
мнѣ: dat. and loc. of я.
могила, *a grave.*
мой, моя, моё, *my*: nom. plur. мои.
мокрый, *wet.*
молитва, *prayer.*
молиться (по-молиться), *to pray.*
молнія, *lightning.*
молодой, —ая, —ое, *young.*
молодость, —и, f., *youth.*
молчаливый, *silent.*
мольба, *prayer.*
море, —я, *sea.*
мостовая, *pavement.*
мракъ, —а, *darkness.*
мужикъ, —а, *peasant.*
мужчина, m., *man.*
мука, *torment.*
мусульманъ, *Moslem.*
мутный, *turbid.*
мчаться (по-мчаться), *to hasten*: pres. ind. мчусь, мчишься.
мы: pl. of я.
мысль, —и, f., *thought.*
мышь, —и, f., *mouse.*
мѣсто, *place.*
мѣсяцъ, *moon.*
мѣшокъ, —ка, *sack.*

на, prep. with loc. or acc., *on, in, to, on to, for*; на яву, *in a waking state.*

на-бѣга́ть (на-бѣжа́ть), *to run towards.*

на-води́ть (на-вести́), *to bring on.*

на-всегда́, *for ever.*

на-го́рный, *on the mountains.*

нагота́, *nakedness.*

надёжда, *hope.*

надъ (and на́до), prep. with instr., *over.*

на-единѣ́, adv., *alone together.*

на́ми: instr. of мы.

намъ: dat. of мы.

на-перeко́ръ, *in defiance of.*

на-пи́саный, *written, decreed.*

на-пи́тывать (на-пита́ть), *to saturate.*

на-пои́ть: see пои́ть.

напра́сно, *in vain.*

на-пѣ́въ, *a tune.*

наро́дъ, —а, *people, nation.*

на-слажда́ться (на-слади́ться), *to enjoy oneself.*

на-слѣ́дникъ, *heir.*

на-става́ть (на-ста́ть), *to arrive.*

насъ: acc. of мы.

начина́ть (нача́ть), *to begin.*

нашъ, —а, —е, *our, ours.*

не, *not.*

небе́сный, *of heaven.*

не́бо, *heaven, sky*: pl. небеса́, небе́съ.

невзго́да, *misfortune.*

не-ви́нный, *innocent.*

него́ = его́.

не-да́вно, *lately.*

не-до-сту́пный, *inaccessible.*

неду́гъ, —а, *sickness.*

не-и́стовый, *furious.*

ней: loc. of она́.

нейти́ (for не идти́), *not to go.*

нему́: dat. of онъ.

нёмъ: loc. of онъ.

не-побѣди́мый, *invincible.*

не-пого́да, *bad weather.*

не-поко́рный, *disobedient.*

не-поро́чный, *free from vice.*

не-пра́вда, *untruth.*

не-проница́емый, *impenetrable.*

не-ро́вный, *uneven.*

нести́сь (по-нести́сь), *to rush, fly.*

ни, negative particle, *neither, nor; not even.*

ни-когда́, *never.*

ни-кто́, *no one.*

нимъ = имъ.

ни́ми = и́ми.

ни-чего́, *nothing, not at all.*

ни́щій, *a beggar.*

но, *but.*

ново-рождённый, *new-born.*

но́вый, *new.*

нога́, *foot, leg.*

ночно́й, —а́я, —о́е, *of the night.*

ночь, —и, *night.*

но́ша, —и, *burden.*

ну, interj., *well.*

нужда́, *need*.
ны́нче, *to-day*.
ны́нѣ, *now*.
нѣ́га, *softness*.
нѣ́жный, *tender*.
нѣтъ, *no, not*.

о, interj., *o, oh!*
обветша́лый, *dilapidated*.
об-вива́ть (об-ви́ть), *to wrap round*.
об-вѣ́ять, *to fan all round*.
оби́тель, —и, f., *dwelling*.
о́блакъ, *a cloud*.
об-лега́ть (об-ле́чь), *to surround*.
об-лета́ть (об-летѣ́ть), *to fly over*.
обма́нъ, *deceit*.
обо́и, m. pl., *wall-paper*.
образо́къ, —ка́, *little image*.
объ (and о́бо), prep. with loc., *about*.
о-гля́дываться (о-гляну́ться), *to look all round*.
огнево́й, —а́я, —о́е, *fiery*.
огнь: see ого́нь.
ого́нь, огня́, m., *fire*.
огра́да, *railings*.
о-даря́ть (о-дари́ть), *to present*.
оди́нъ, одна́, одно́, *a, one, alone*.
одна́ко, *however*.
одръ, *bed*.

о-дѣва́ть (о-дѣ́ть), *to clothe, cover*.
о-жида́ть, *to wait for*.
о-забо́ченъ, *concerned*: perf. pass. part. of о-забо́титься.
о́зеро, *a lake*.
о-зира́ться (о-зрѣ́ться), *to look about*.
окно́, *window*.
о́ко, *eye*: pl. о́чи.
око́шко, *window*.
о-ку́танный, *wrapped up*.
о-мрача́ть (о-мрачи́ть), *to darken*.
о-мы́тый, *drenched*.
она́: fem. of онъ.
онъ, она́, оно́, *he, she, it*: pl. они́, онѣ́, *they*.
опа́сный, *dangerous*.
о-печа́лить: see печа́лить.
о-по́мниться, *to become conscious*.
о-пуска́ть(о-пусти́ть), *to lower*.
опя́ть, *again*.
орёлъ, орла́, *eagle*.
о-роша́ть (о-роси́ть), *to wet*.
о-свѣжа́ть (о-свѣжи́ть), *to refresh*.
о-слабѣ́лъ: see слабѣ́ть.
остава́ться (оста́ться), *to remain*: остаю́сь, остаёшься (оста́нусь, оста́нешься).
оставля́ть (оста́вить), *to leave*.
от-выќать (от-вы́кнуть), *to grow unaccustomed*.

отвѣ́тъ, *answer.*

от-дава́ть (от-да́ть), *to surrender.*

оте́цъ, отца́, *father.*

о-тира́ть (о-тере́ть), *to wipe.*

от-ло́гій, *sloping.*

отра́да, *consolation.*

от-река́ться (от-ре́чься), *to deny.*

от-ту́да, *from there.*

от-шумѣ́ть, *to cease sounding.*

отъ, prep. with gen., *from.*

очаро́вывать (очарова́ть), *to enchant.*

о́чень, *very, very much.*

о́чи: see о́ко.

па́дать (у-па́сть), *to fall.*

па́поротникъ, *fern.*

па́рить, *to scorch.*

па́смурный, *dull.*

пасту́шій, —шья, —шье, *of a shepherd.*

пе́рвый, *first.*

пе́редъ, prep. with instr., *in front of, before.*

пере-жива́ть (пере-жи́ть), *to survive.*

пере-крёстокъ, *cross-road.*

пере-носи́ть (пере-нести́), *to transport.*

песо́къ, —ка́, *sand.*

пёсъ, *a dog.*

печа́лить (о-печа́лить), *to distress.*

печа́льный, *sad.*

писа́ть (на-писа́ть), *to write.*

пить (вы́-пить), *to drink*: pres. ind. пью, пьёшь.

пла́кать (за-пла́кать), *to weep.*

плащъ, —а́, *cloak.*

плеска́ть (плесну́ть), *to splash*: pres. ind. плещу́, пле́щешь.

плечо́, —а́, *shoulder.*

плохо́й, —а́я, —о́е, *bad.*

плугъ, —а, *a plough.*

по, prep. with acc., dat. or loc., *on, through, by, according to.*

по-бы́ть, *to be for a time.*

по-ви́съ: see висѣ́ть.

по-води́ть (по-вести́), *to start off.*

по-вѣ́рить: see вѣ́рить.

по-гаша́ть (по-гаси́ть), *to extinguish.*

по-ги́бнетъ: see ги́бнуть.

по-го́да, *weather.*

по-гружённый, *absorbed.*

под-вози́ть (под-везти́), *to carry up.*

под-ку́пленный, *bribed.*

под-нима́ть (под-ня́ть), *to raise.*

по-дру́жка, *dear friend (female).*

под-свѣ́чникъ, *candlestick.*

под-ходи́ть, *to approach.*

подъ, prep. with instr., *under; to the sound of.*

поётъ: pres. of пѣть.

позорный, *shameful.*

поить (на-поить), *to saturate, give drink to.*

поймётъ: see понимать.

пойти, *to proceed*: pres. ind. пойду, —ёшь.

пока...не, *until.*

по-кидать (по-кинуть), *to forsake.*

поклонникъ, *worshipper.*

поклонъ, *greeting.*

покой, —оя, *rest.*

покорять (покорить), *to conquer.*

по-крывать (по-крыть), *to cover.*

пол-день, полу-дня, m., *noon.*

поле, —я, pl. поля, *field.*

ползти (по-ползти), *to creep*: pres. ind. ползу, —зёшь.

полкъ, —а, *regiment.*

полно-властно, adv., *with full power.*

пол-ночный, *of midnight.*

полный, *full*; полно мнѣ, *I have had enough.*

по-ложить: see класть.

полу-прозрачный, *half-transparent.*

по-мнить (вс-по-мнить), *to remember.*

по-мѣстье, *estate.*

по-нимать (по-нять, по-йму, по-ймёшь), *to understand.*

понятный, *intelligible.*

по-плакать, *to weep a little.*

пора, *time, season, the right time.*

по-раждать (по-родить), *to bring forth.*

порокъ, —а, *vice.*

поруганный, *reviled.*

по-слалъ: see по-сылать.

по-слушливый, *obedient.*

по-слушно, *obediently.*

послѣдній, —яя, —ее, *last.*

по-смотрѣть: see смотрѣть.

поститься, *to fast.*

по-сылать (по-слать), *to send.*

по-течь, *to start off.*

по-томъ, *afterwards.*

по-тухать (по-тухнуть), *to be extinguished.*

потъ, *sweat.*

по-утру, *in the morning.*

походъ, *campaign.*

по-цѣловать: see цѣловать.

поцѣлуй, *a kiss.*

почва, *soil, ground.*

по-шли: imperative of по-слать: see слать.

по-ѣдешь: see ѣхать.

поютъ: pres. of пѣть.

по-являться (по-явиться), *to appear.*

правда, *truth.*

право, adv., *truly.*

пре-давать (пре-дать), *to surrender.*

пре́до = пе́редъ.
предѣлъ, *frontier, kingdom.*
пре́жній, —яя, —ее, *former.*
прекра́сный, *pretty.*
пре-ступле́нье, *crime.*
при, prep. with loc., *in presence of.*
при-вѣ́тъ, *greeting.*
придётъ: see при-ходи́ть.
при-знава́ться (при-зна́ться), *to confess.*
при-зракъ, *a vision.*
при-зы́вной, adj., *summoning.*
при-носи́ть (при-нести́), *to bring, fetch.*
при-ро́да, *nature.*
при-слу́шиваться, *to listen attentively.*
при-сыла́ть (при-сла́ть), *to send.*
при-ходи́ть (придти́), *to arrive.*
при-хо́дъ, *arrival.*
прі-у-молка́ть (прі-у-мо́лкнуть), *to be silent.*
про, prep. with acc., *concerning.*
про-бива́ться (про-би́ться), *to break through.*
про-води́ть (про-вести́), *to spend (of time).*
про-вожа́ть, *to see off.*
про-во́рный, *active.*
про-гова́ривать (про-говори́ть), *to articulate.*
про-зра́чный, *transparent.*
про-йдётъ: see про-ходи́ть.
про-клина́ть (про-кля́сть), *to curse.*
про-лива́ть (про-ли́ть), *to shed.*
про-мелька́ть (про-мелькну́ть), *to flash past.*
про-мока́ть (про-мо́кнуть), *to be wet through.*
про-мча́ться, *to speed past.*
проро́къ, —а, *prophet.*
проси́ться, *to ask to go.*
про-спа́ть, *to over-sleep.*
про-хла́да, *coolness.*
про-хла́дный, *cool.*
про-ходи́ть (про-йти́), *to pass by, walk on.*
прочь, adv., *away, on.*
про-шла́: past tense of про-йдти́.
проща́льный, *of farewell.*
пти́ца, *bird.*
пти́чій, —чья, —чье, *of a bird.*
пу́ля, *a bullet.*
пуска́й: imperative of пуска́ть.
пуска́ть (пусти́ть), *to let, to throw.*
пусто́й, —а́я, —о́е, *empty.*
пусты́нный, *uninhabited.*
пусты́ня, *desert, wilderness.*
пусть: imperative of пусти́ть.
пу́тникъ, *traveller.*
путь, —и́, m., *way, journey.*

пу́ще, adv., *more.*
пыла́ть (за-пыла́ть), *to flame.*
пыль, —и, f., *dust.*
пьётъ: from пить.
пѣ́на, *foam.*
пѣ́сенка, *a little song.*
пѣ́сня, *a song.*
пѣть (с-пѣть), *to sing.*
пята́, *heel.*

рабо́тать (по-рабо́тать), *to work.*
ра́бскій, *of a slave.*
рабъ, —а́, *slave.*
ра́вный, *equal*; всё равно́, *all the same.*
рожда́ться (роди́ться), *to be born.*
раз-би́тый, *worn-out, broken in pieces.*
раз-вра́тъ, —а, *debauchery.*
раз-дава́ться (раз-да́ться), *to spread, to be heard.*
раз-да́вливатъ (раз-дави́ть), *to crush.*
раз-дира́ть (раз-о-дра́ть), *to cleave.*
раз-до́лье, *expanse, room.*
раз-ду́мье, *doubt.*
раз-ли́чный, *different.*
ра́зный, *various.*
раз-о-сла́лъ: see раз-сыла́ть.
раз-о-шью́: see рас-шива́ть
раз-раста́ть (раз-рости́), *to grow strongly.*
раз-рыва́ться (раз-о-рва́ться), *to be torn asunder.*
раз-ска́зъ, —а, *tale.*
раз-ска́зывать (разсказа́ть), *to tell.*
раз-става́ться (раз-ста́ться), *to part.*
раз-сыла́ть (раз-о-сла́ть), *to deal out.*
раз-сѣва́ть (раз-сѣ́ять), *to disperse.*
разъ, —а, *time*; ни ра́зу, *not even once.*
ра́на, *wound.*
ра́ненъ, *wounded.*
ра́нить (по-ра́нить), *to wound.*
ра́нній, —яя, —ее, *early.*
раскалённый, *red-hot.*
рас-топя́сь: see топи́ть.
рас-шива́ть (раз-о-ши́ть), *to embroider.*
ревни́вый, *jealous.*
робкій, *timid.*
роди́лся: see рожда́ться.
родно́й, —а́я, —о́е, *native, own.*
родъ, *birth, family*; на роду́, *at birth.*
роси́стый, *dewy.*
роско́шный, *luxuriant.*
ро́скошь, —и, f., *luxury.*
ро́ща, *a wood.*
ружьё, —ья́, n., *gun.*
рука́, *hand, arm.*
румя́нецъ, —ца, *red colour.*

румя́ный, *ruddy*.
Ру́сскій, *Russian*.
Русь, —и, f., *Russia*.
руче́й, —чья́, *stream*.
рыба́чій, —чья, —чье, *of fishermen*.
рѣ́звый, *impetuous*.
рѣка́, *river*.
рядъ, —а, *train, line*.

са́бля, —и, *sword*.
сади́ться (сѣсть), *to sit down*.
садъ, —а, *garden*.
са́льный, *of tallow*.
самъ, —а́, —о́, *-self*: plur. са́ми: самъ-собо́ю, *alone*.
свобо́дный, *free*.
сводъ, —а, *vault, roof*.
свой, —оя́, —оё, *mine, thine, his*.
свѣ́жій, *fresh*.
свѣти́ть (по-свѣти́ть), *to shine*.
свѣ́тлый, *bright*.
свѣ́точъ, *a torch*.
свѣтъ, *world, light*.
свѣча́, *candle*.
с-вя́заный, *tied together*.
свято́й,—а́я,—о́е, *sacred, holy*.
с-гиба́ть (со-гну́ть), *to bend*.
с-двига́ть (с-дви́нуть), *to knit (the brows)*.
с-дѣлать: see дѣлать.
себя́, себѣ́, собо́й, reflexive pron., *oneself, myself, thyself* etc.
сей, сія́, сіё, *this*.
селе́ніе, —я, *settlement*.
семьи́шка, *little family*.
серде́чный, *of the heart*.
се́рдце, *heart*.
серена́да, *serenade*.
си́день, —дня, *a sitter*.
сидѣ́ть (по-сидѣ́ть), *to be sitting*.
си́ла, *power*.
сини́ца, *blue bird*.
си́рый, *bereaved*.
сихъ: gen. plur. of сей.
сія́ніе, *glitter*.
скажи́: imperative of сказа́ть.
сказа́ть: see говори́ть.
ска́зка, *fairy-tale*.
ска́зывать (сказа́ть), *to tell*.
скака́ть (по-скака́ть), *to gallop*.
скала́, *rock*.
сквози́ть, *to peep through, let light through*.
сквозно́й, —а́я, —о́е, *transparent*.
сквозь, prep. with acc., *through*.
с-кла́дывать (с-ложи́ть), *to fold*.
с-клоня́ться (с-клони́ться), *to stoop*.
ско́лько, *how many, how much*.
ско́рбный, *sorrowful*.
скорбь, —и, f., *trouble*.
ско́ро, *soon*; какъ ско́ро, *as soon as*.

с-крыва́ться (с-кры́ться), *to hide oneself.*
ску́дный, *beggarly.*
скупо́й, —а́я, —о́е, *barren.*
скуча́ть (по-скуча́ть), *to be homesick.*
слабѣ́ть (о-слабѣ́ть), *to grow weak.*
сла́ва, *glory.*
сла́вить (про-сла́вить), *to glorify.*
сла́дкій, *sweet.*
сла́дость, —и, f., *sweetness.*
слать (по-сла́ть), *to send.*
слеза́, *tear*: pl. слёзы.
сло́вно, *like, as if.*
с-ложи́вши: see скла́дывать.
слу́шать (по-слу́шать), *to listen.*
слы́шно, neut. adj., *audible.*
сме́ртный, *deadly, of death.*
смерть, —и, f., *death.*
с-мире́нный, *humble.*
смола́, *resin.*
смотри́тель, *post-master.*
смотрѣ́ть (по-смотрѣ́ть), *to look.*
смѣ́ло, adv., *boldly.*
с-но́ва, adv., *afresh.*
с-носи́ть (с-нести́), *to endure.*
снѣ: loc. of сонъ.
снѣ́гъ, —а, *snow.*
снѣ́жный, *snowy.*
со-бира́ть (со-бра́ть), *to collect.*
со-гбе́нный, *bent, bowed.*
со-гну́ть: see с-гиба́ть.
со-зна́тельный, *conscious.*
сойдёшь: see с-ходи́ть.
со́колъ, *falcon.*
со-кро́йся: imperat. of скры́ться.
со́лнечный, *of the sun.*
со́лнце, *sun.*
солове́й, —вья́, *nightingale.*
соло́ма, *straw.*
со́нно, adv., *sleepily.*
со́нный, *asleep, sleeping.*
сонъ, сна, *sleep, a dream.*
сосѣ́дка, *female neighbour.*
сосѣ́дъ, —а, *neighbour*: n. plur. сосѣ́ди.
со-храни́тъ: see храни́ть.
спаса́ть (спасти́), *to save.*
спать (по-спа́ть), *to sleep*: сплю, спишь etc.
спи: imperative of спать.
с-пой: imperative of с-пѣть.
споко́йный, *quiet, calm.*
с-пою́: pres. ind. of с-пѣть: see пѣть.
спра́шивать (спроси́ть), *to ask.*
спроси́ть: see спра́шивать.
с-пуска́ться (с-пусти́ться), *to descend.*
спя́щій: pres. part. of спать.
среди́, prep. with gen., *amid.*
ста́вить (по-ста́вить), *to place.*
Стамбу́лъ, *Stambul, Constantinople.*
станови́ться (стать), *to become, begin.*

ста́ну: pres. of стать.
ста́нція, *a post-house.*
старина́, *old times.*
стари́нный, *old-fashioned.*
стару́ха, *old woman.*
стару́шка, *old woman.*
ста́рый, *old.*
стать, *to become, begin*: ста́ну, ста́нешь; past ста́лъ.
с-тека́ть (с-течь), *to exude.*
степь, —и, f., *steppe, prairie.*
столбъ, —а́, *pillar, post.*
стоя́ть (по-стоя́ть), *to stand.*
страда́ть (по-страда́ть), *to suffer.*
страна́, *country.*
стра́стно, *passionately.*
страсть, —и, f., *passion.*
страхъ, —а, *fear.*
стре́мя, —е́мени, n., *stirrup.*
струи́ться, *to flow.*
струя́, *jet, flow.*
стрѣла́, *arrow.*
сту́кнуть, *to tick.*
ступа́ть (ступи́ть), *to walk.*
ступе́нь, —е́ни, f., *step.*
стуча́ть (по-стуча́ть), *to knock.*
стѣна́, *wall.*
судьба́, *fortune.*
суро́вый, *hard, harsh.*
с-ходи́ть (со-йти́), *to descend.*
сча́стіе, *happiness.*
съ (and со), prep. with instr. or gen., (1) *with*; (2) *from.*
сы́тый, *sufficiently fed.*
сѣ́веръ, *the North.*
сѣде́льце, *a saddle.*
сѣлъ: see сади́ться.
сѣнь, —и, f., *tent.*
сѣ́рый, *grey.*
сѣ́товать, *to complain.*
сѣть, —и, f., *a net.*

таи́нственный, *mysterious.*
та́йно, *secretly.*
тако́въ, —ва́, —во́, *such.*
тако́й, —а́я, —о́е, *such.*
такъ, *thus, so, merely*; та́къ же, *in the same way.*
талисма́нъ, *talisman, charm.*
тамъ, *there.*
тащи́ть (по-тащи́ть), *to draw.*
тверди́ть, *to repeat.*
твёрдый, *firm.*
твой, —ая́, —оё, *thine.*
тебя́: gen. and acc. of ты.
текли́: from течь.
телѣ́га, *a cart.*
тёмный, *dark.*
тепе́рь, *now.*
тёплый, *warm.*
теплѣ́е, adv., *more warmly.*
терно́вый, *of thorns.*
терпѣ́ть (по-терпѣ́ть), *to endure.*
течь (по-течь), *to flow.*
тигръ, *tiger.*
ти́хій, —ая, —ое, *still.*
ти́хо, adv., *quietly, peacefully.*
тихо́нько, adv., *with no noise.*

тишина́, *stillness.*
тле-тво́рный, *pestilential.*
то: neut. of тотъ: то...то, *at one time...at another.*
тобо́ю or тобо́й: instr. of ты.
толпа́, *host, crowd.*
толпи́ться (с-толпи́ться), *to come crowding.*
то́лько, *only.*
томи́ться (ис-томи́ться), *to grow weary.*
тому́: dat. of тотъ.
то́нкій, *fine, delicate.*
топи́ть (рас-топи́ть), *to melt.*
торжество́, *triumph.*
торжествова́ть, *to triumph.*
торопли́вый, *hasty.*
тоска́, *grief.*
тотъ, та, то, demonstr. pron., *that.*
точи́ть (на-точи́ть), *to sharpen.*
то́чно, *exactly.*
трава́, *grass.*
трезво́нъ, *peal, carol.*
тре́звый, *sober.*
тре́петъ, *tremor.*
тропа́, *path.*
тростни́къ, *reed-bed.*
труба́, *pipe.*
труди́ться (по-труди́ться), *to labour.*
трудъ, —а́, *labour.*
тря́скій, *jolty.*
ту: acc. fem. of тотъ.
тума́нъ, —а, *mist.*
ту́ча, —и, *rain-cloud.*
ты, *thou*: pl. вы.
ты́сяча, *a thousand.*
тьма, *a myriad.*
тѣ: plur. of тотъ.
тѣмъ: instr. of тотъ.
тѣнь, f., *shadow.*
тя́гостный, *painful.*
тяжело́, *heavily.*

у, prep. with gen., *belonging to, near.*
у-би́тый, *crushed.*
убо́гій, *crippled.*
у-бѣга́ть (у-бѣжа́ть), *to run away.*
у-влечённый, *carried away.*
у-вя́дшій, *faded.*
угрю́мый, *sullen.*
у-дава́ться (у-да́ться), *to succeed.*
удруча́ть (удручи́ть), *to oppress.*
уже́ (and ужъ), *already, by this time; surely.*
у-знава́ть (у-зна́ть), *to learn.*
у-кра́дкой, adv., *by stealth.*
у-крыва́ться (у-кры́ться), *to shelter* (intr.).
улы́бка, *a smile.*
у-мира́ть (у-мере́ть), *to die.*
у-мыва́ться (у-мы́ться), *to wash oneself.*
у-мча́ть, *to carry off.*

у-носи́ть (у-нести́), *to bear away.*
у-ны́лый, *doleful.*
у-паду́: see па́дать.
у-пива́ться (у-пи́ться), *to intoxicate oneself.*
упру́гій, *supple.*
урага́нъ, *hurricane.*
у-с-поко́енный, *calmed.*
уста́, pl. n., *lips.*
у-ства́ть (у-ста́ть), *to grow weary.*
у-ста́лый, *tired.*
у-стремля́ть (у-стреми́ть), *to direct.*
у́тка, *a duck.*
у-томля́ть (у-томи́ть), *to wear out.*
у́тро, *morning.*
утро́ба, *bosom.*
у-тѣша́ться (у-тѣ́шиться), *to be comforted.*

фонта́нъ, —а, *spring, fountain.*

хла́дный = холо́дный, *cold.*
хладъ = хо́лодъ.
хлопота́ть (по-хлопота́ть), *to fuss.*
ходи́ть (с-ходи́ть), *to go, walk, move.*
хозя́инъ, *master of the house.*
холо́дный, *cold.*
хо́лодъ, *cold.*
хорово́дъ, *train.*
хотѣ́ть (за-хотѣ́ть), *to wish.*
хотя́ (and хоть), *although.*
хохота́ть (за-хохота́ть), *to laugh loud.*
храни́ть (со-храни́ть), *to preserve.*
храпѣ́ть, *to snore.*
хребе́тъ, —та́, *back-bone.*
хруста́льный, *of crystal.*

цари́ть, *to reign.*
царь, —я́, *king.*
цвѣсти́ (за-цвѣсти́), *to bloom.*
цѣлова́ть (по-цѣлова́ть), *to kiss.*
цѣлый, *whole.*
цѣпь, —и, f., *chain.*

часово́й, *sentinel.*
часъ, —а, *hour.*
ча́хлый, *plague-stricken.*
ча́ша, *cup.*
чего́: gen. of что.
чело́, *forehead.*
человѣ́къ, *man.*
че́резъ, prep. with acc., *through.*
черезчу́ръ, adv., *beyond measure.*
чёрный, *black.*
чернѣ́ть, *to grow dark.*
че́рпать (черпну́ть), *to draw, drink.*
че́стно, adv., *honourably.*

Чече́нъ, *mountaineer.*
чи́стый, *pure, clean.*
что, *that; why?*
что̀, *that which.*
что́-бы or чтобъ, *that.*
чу́вствовать (по-чу́вствовать), *to feel.*
чу́ждый, *foreign.*
чужо́й, —а́я, —о́е, *foreign.*
чуть, adv., *hardly.*
чу́ять (по-чу́ять), *to scent out.*

шага́ть (шагну́ть), *to step.*
шала́шъ, —а́, *hut.*
ша́ткій, *shaky.*
шёлъ, *he walked*: past tense of идти́.
шепта́ть (шепну́ть), *to whisper.*
шкапъ, —а, *cupboard.*
широ́кій, *broad.*
шла, *she walked*: past tense of идти́.
шлютъ: 3rd pers. plur., pres. ind. of слать.
шолкъ, *silk.*
шумъ, —а, *noise.*
шумѣ́ть (за-шумѣ́ть), *to make a noise.*

ѣ́хать (по-ѣ́хать), ѣ́ду, ѣ́дешь, *to go (not on foot).*

э́тотъ, э́та, э́то, *this.*

югъ, *the South.*
ю́ность, —и, f., *youth.*

я, меня́, мнѣ, мно́ю or мной, *I, me.*
яву: see на.
ядови́тый, *poisonous.*
ядъ, —а, *poison.*
я́ркій, *bright.*
я́сный, *clear, bright.*

For EU product safety concerns, contact us at Calle de José Abascal, 56–1°, 28003 Madrid, Spain or eugpsr@cambridge.org.

www.ingramcontent.com/pod-product-compliance
Ingram Content Group UK Ltd.
Pitfield, Milton Keynes, MK11 3LW, UK
UKHW012333130625
459647UK00009B/263

* 9 7 8 1 1 0 7 6 4 6 9 2 6 *